Praise for *Religion, Politics, and Polarization*

"The ideological polarization of our political parties is one of the most important and defining characteristics of contemporary American politics, both in the mass public and within our elected institutions. In this concise volume, the authors provide an excellent analysis of the various ways in which religion interacts with partisan affiliation to influence the polarized voting behavior of members of Congress over the last several decades. This book is highly recommended for anyone seeking a more comprehensive understanding of the intersection of religion and politics in modern American society."
—**Benjamin R. Knoll**, Centre College

"This book is an indispensable guide to the role religion has played, and is playing, in the U.S. Congress. In recent years, scholars have spent a lot of time and energy understanding the religion of voters, but far less research has been devoted to religion among lawmakers. William V. D'Antonio, Steven A. Tuch, and Josiah R. Baker fill in this gap—demonstrating that making law is often a matter of faith." —**David E. Campbell**, University of Notre Dame

"This is an important study for understanding the effects of religious belief and affiliation on the oppositional dynamics and processes of American politics and political institutions and on the competing visions of the good society that underlie those conflicts. The authors show that some common understandings of conflictual American political phenomena—articulated in such metaphors as 'culture wars'—either have less empirical evidence to support them than might be imagined or require tempering and nuancing to be useful for understanding significant aspects of those phenomena. It is in the relationship between party affiliation and religious affiliation that we find perhaps the most politically potent and divisive correlations." —**Thomas Heilke**, University of Kansas

Religion, Politics, and Polarization

How Religiopolitical Conflict Is Changing Congress and American Democracy

William V. D'Antonio, Steven A. Tuch,
and Josiah R. Baker

ROWMAN & LITTLEFIELD PUBLISHERS, INC.
Lanham • Boulder • New York • Toronto • Plymouth, UK

Published by Rowman & Littlefield Publishers, Inc.
A wholly owned subsidiary of The Rowman & Littlefield Publishing Group, Inc.
4501 Forbes Boulevard, Suite 200, Lanham, Maryland 20706
www.rowman.com

10 Thornbury Road, Plymouth PL6 7PP, United Kingdom

British Library Cataloguing in Publication Information Available

Library of Congress Cataloging-in-Publication Data
D'Antonio, William V.
  Religion, politics, and polarization : how religiopolitical conflict is changing Congress and American democracy / William V. D'Antonio, Steven A. Tuch, and Josiah R. Baker.
    pages cm
  Includes bibliographical references and index.
  ISBN 978-1-4422-2107-9 (cloth : alk. paper) — ISBN 978-1-4422-2108-6 (electronic)
1. United States. Congress. 2. Legislators—United States. 3. Religion and politics—United States. 4. Church and state—United States. I. Title.
  JK1021.D35 2013
  328.7309'045—dc23
                                                              2012044709

™ The paper used in this publication meets the minimum requirements of American National Standard for Information Sciences—Permanence of Paper for Printed Library Materials, ANSI/NISO Z39.48-1992.

Printed in the United States of America

Contents

Contents

Preface and Acknowledgments

In this book we attempt to unravel the complex relationship between religion and political party in order to better understand how their confluence has impacted roll call voting in the U.S. Congress over the past four decades. Our primary goal is to examine whether—and if so how—religion and party have combined to shape the growing partisanship in Congress over this period and, secondarily, to determine if these cleavages are also reflected in public opinion polls.

Our study is an extension of the work of such scholars as Benson and Williams (1982) and James Davison Hunter (1991, 1994), to whom we owe a special debt of intellectual gratitude. In their landmark study, Benson and Williams demonstrated that many members of Congress held strong religious beliefs that influenced how they voted. Hunter identified the emerging culture wars as involving different visions of the "good society." We hope that our study builds on these scholars' seminal contributions by clarifying how religion and party have shaped congressional voting patterns and public opinion trends over the last four decades.

Many people and organizations played key roles in bringing this project to completion. In the early years support was provided by the Life Cycle Institute of Catholic University and more recently by its successor, the Institute for Policy Research and Catholic Studies. We are indebted to Stephen Schneck, the current director of the Institute, for his generous support. The authors also gratefully acknowledge research support from the joint American Sociological Association/National Science Foundation Fund for the Advancement of the Discipline and the Columbian College of Arts and Sciences at The George Washington University. John K. White generously shared with us his extensive knowledge of the confluence of electoral politics and religion and helped us refine our thinking at several stages of the project. We also thank our research assistants for their many contributions, not least of which was the compilation of a dataset that spanned several decades of congressional voting: Karla Yoder, Todd Scribner, Christopher Roelofs, Rosemary Chien, and Matthew Beben. We are also grateful for the administrative assistance of Mary Anne Eley, Ann Kaspryzak, Andrew Lautz, and Woinishet Negash.

A special word of appreciation is due to Anne Roan Thomas for her help with literature reviews and the drafting of parts of chapters 2 and 3.

We are also indebted to a number of colleagues who provided critical commentary on various parts of the manuscript. Barbara Brown Zikmund read chapters 1–4; Nancy Ammerman read chapter 2; and Anthony Pogorelc, Greg Smith, Charles Davis, and Bob Antonio read parts of several chapters. Despite these colleagues' contributions, we remain solely responsible for any remaining errors.

We are pleased to recognize the support provided by Rowman & Littlefield Publishers throughout all phases of the project. Sarah Stanton recognized early on the potential of the manuscript. We are also grateful to Jin Yu for editorial assistance and to Patricia Stevenson for her patience and commitment to moving our manuscript along in production.

Finally, to Lorraine and Sandra, words of deep appreciation for their unwavering support and patience, and to Robert A. Baker III, whose encouragement helped Josiah Baker complete his dissertation even as he was coauthoring this book.

1

Setting the Stage

Culture Wars, Religion, and Congress

It is the truth of the hour: Washington—or, if *you* prefer, "the system"—is in extremis, trapped in a depressing cycle of partisan dysfunctionality. There is something to this, but the broad indictment of the capital and its culture too often fails to include the government's co-conspirators: WE the People. . . . In fact, the system that has been declared unworkable in op-ed land is working the way it was supposed to work. It is a sign of success, not failure, when things move slowly, or not at all.

—Jon Meacham, "We Are All Co-Conspirators Now" (2010)

Pulitzer Prize–winning author and political pundit Jon Meacham argued that Washington was and is an expression of the will of the people. That is, we the people do not want to change the things that benefit us, especially if it will cost us money. Meacham quoted one of his friends as saying, "A lot of Americans have the souls of Democrats and the pocketbooks of Republicans" (Meacham 2010, 3).

Did Meacham really put into words what ails us? Or is it more than a bit simplistic to say that Americans have the souls of Democrats and the pocketbooks of Republicans? Was Meacham speaking more about the voting public than about the people who are elected to carry out their will? Are members of the U.S. Congress really more alike than they would have us believe? Do Republican Catholics have Democratic souls, while Democratic Catholics have Republican pocketbooks? Regarding Jews in Congress, how would Meacham's claim hold up in the 2010 Senate, where most Jews were Democrats, and in the 2010 House, where there was only one Republican among some thirty Jews? These are the kinds of questions that led us to embark on this study.

IN THE BEGINNING

Our story begins in the year 2000 when we became curious about how religious affiliation might influence congressional voting on abortion, housing for the poor, the death penalty, and a variety of other moral and social issues. The story ends with the vote on the Obama administration's health care bill on March 21, 2010, following a hectic week of verbal skirmishes about how best to protect life. The abortion issue, very much alive ten years earlier, was still divisive during the resolution of the health care bill.[1]

We were curious about what abortion votes in the House and Senate might look like if we identified members by religion as well as party. That curiosity gradually led us to compare votes on abortion with roll call votes on all key issues from 1969 to 2010. In the process, we found a host of interesting examples of stability and change, including change in the denominational makeup of the two parties. With these examples and data, we were ready to put Meacham's claim into a larger context. In doing so, we addressed a number of questions:

- What changes have taken place in the denominational makeup of the U.S. House and Senate during the last half century? Did the religious changes affect both parties or just one, especially regarding voting on key legislative items? A measure of the importance of the changes would be seen in these votes.
- What changes took place in roll call voting during the past forty years? Our examination includes abortion votes and roll calls on an array of issues, such as military expenditures, taxes, welfare programs, and (in appendix A) civil rights.

A review of the literature led to the question of whether, in fact, there was substance to the claim that our society was experiencing a culture war and whether it might be reflected in House and Senate votes during this period. In other words, the culture wars hypothesis, formulated by Hunter in 1991 with its two distinct visions of the good society, raised the question of whether congressional roll call voting in the House and Senate was being impacted. Further, what was the relationship between the growing evidence of polarization within and between parties and the culture war thesis?

Would we find that polarization was anchored in the culture war, as witnessed by roll call votes not only on moral values issues like abortion but also on issues like housing for the poor, raising the minimum wage, and Medicare reform that are increasingly said by religious leaders to be moral issues? What role did religion play in the policy directions of the two parties? Would it be possible to determine whether and to what extent religious teachings and values were becoming part of party ideology? Finally, we asked what exactly the term *polarization* meant. How was it to be measured? Was it just a phenomenon of cross-party voting, or was it also to be found within parties? And what would be its consequences over time?

For almost four decades now, issues such as abortion, homosexuality, and the nature of marriage have competed for public attention with health care, war, terrorism, and the growing inequity between the income of the working and middle classes and that of bankers, Wall Street brokers, and corporate CEOs. Was the public really more concerned about moral issues like abortion than socioeconomic issues like feeding or housing the poor that were not seen as having the same moral importance? What was the level of involvement of religious groups in these issues, and how might religion be shaping the policymaking process in Congress?

BENSON AND WILLIAMS

"In nearly all past studies that have inquired into the identity, activity, and motivations of Congress, one area has remained almost entirely unexplored: the area of religion," said Peter Benson and Dorothy Williams in their pathbreaking book *Religion on Capitol Hill* (Benson and Williams 1982). They used an extensive array of instruments to measure the religious beliefs, values, attitudes, and behavior of eighty members of Congress, selected by a specially designed random sample of the 535 members of the House and Senate. Their major findings provided an important point of departure for our study. Consider those findings: Nearly all members of Congress affirmed a belief in God; members of Congress were no less religious than the people they served; political conservatives were no more religious than political liberals; Evangelical Christians were not a united conservative political force; and the majority of the eighty members believed that God is both transcendent and immanent, God is involved in the course of history, scripture is more than myth and allegory, scripture may not be perfectly accurate in every detail, Jesus was divine and human, there is life after death and in that life individuality is preserved, both heaven and hell exist, and people tend more toward good than toward evil.

Benson and Williams also stated that "three-quarters of the members of the U.S. Congress were genuinely religious, to the point where religion was a definite influence on their thoughts and actions, an integral part of their lives" (1982, 72). Furthermore, according to the two authors, a majority of the eighty members they interviewed acknowledged that their votes were influenced by their religious beliefs and values. Benson and Williams also found it was not possible to predict how members of Congress would vote based solely on their religious affiliation. Among their conclusions, they said,

> Religious belief should join some of the more commonly recognized factors, like party affiliation and constituent pressure, as forces that bear on political behavior. . . . Knowing how members scored on three or four of the religious themes can tell us as much or more about how they will vote than knowing whether they are Republican or Democrat. (164–65)

Unfortunately for our purposes, Benson and Williams presented no information identifying their interviewees either by party or by religion, so we were left with that task. Almost all members list their professed religion in their biographies. The Benson and Williams research took place just before the election of Ronald Reagan in 1980, and the book's publication came two years into the Reagan administration and included a special profile of the New Christian Right, which had emerged with the Reagan election.

Two decades later, the Republican Party had identified itself as the party with strong religious ties. These claims have been supported by public opinion polls showing that among Americans attending church services regularly, Republicans held a distinct partisan advantage.[2] The media have depicted religiousness as going to church regularly and supporting traditional moral values regarding sexuality. These moral values included especially an absolute stand against abortion, abstinence from sexual activity before marriage, and opposition to same-sex marriage. Apparently, concern for the poor and needy or for the common good were not considered moral values by the Republican Party, by the press, or by many members of the Democratic Party.

During this period (1980s and 1990s), social science research focused on the degree of threat posed to the vital center by religious extremes. A brief review of the literature that focused on public opinion and on the people whom the public elected to Congress revealed how little attention was being paid to the role that religion might be playing in the public square.

LITERATURE REVIEW

The late Nelson Polsby had nothing to say about religion in his book *How Congress Evolves*. His focus was on the "social bases of institutional change," and he did not cite religion as one of those social bases (2004). He mentioned Ronald Reagan but made no mention of Reagan's successful wooing of the Evangelicals into the Republican fold in 1980 and the consequences arising from that political move.

Neither the word "religion" nor the name of any specific religion is anywhere to be found in the 2006 book *The Broken Branch*, by the two distinguished congressional scholars Tom Mann and Norm Ornstein (2006). It was not that their analysis was flawed; rather, their focus was elsewhere.

In 2006, Pietro Nivola and David Brady published *Red and Blue Nation: Characteristics and Causes of America's Polarized Politics.* In it, E. J. Dionne (2006) and Alan Wolfe (2006) made and defended the case for the importance of religion in the activities of the U.S. Congress. Wolfe agreed with Dionne's detailed analysis of religion's role in American politics and he added, "When evangelicals began to flex their political muscle in the 1970s, almost no political scientists—and very few journalists—paid them much attention. That we could ignore something so important was, in my opinion, one of the biggest mistakes our fields could have made" (Wolfe 2006, 206).

Meanwhile, other scholars were beginning to build on Benson and Williams with studies of roll call votes. One of the earliest was the article "Holy Roll-Calls: Religious Tradition and Voting Behavior in the U.S. House" by Chris Fastnow, J. Tobin Grant, and Thomas J. Rudolph (1999). In a study of abortion votes in the House of Representatives covering the years 1959–1994, the authors found that "religious affiliation significantly affects specific and general roll call voting behavior, and that religious groups in Congress differ from one another, both within and across parties" (687). They asserted that "our results not only show that religion affects congressional voting, they also suggest the way religion plays a role in congressional decision making." They added, "Religion stands up to the competition of a variety of other theoretically powerful predictors of voting behavior, including party, constituency preferences, and important demographic indicators" (697).

Another example was David Mariott's "Righteous Roll Calls: Religion, Choice, and Morality Politics in the U.S. House and Senate, 1999–2002." Mariott presented the paper at the Midwest Political Science Association conference in April 2005. This study continued on the path of research studying legislative roll call voting in the U.S. House on morality issues such as gay rights and abortion. Mariott compared abortion roll call votes in both the House and Senate over a three-year time span. He tested the hypothesis that there was a significant difference in voting behavior between the two chambers. He found that ideology and party were the strongest indicators of pro-choice voting, with religious affiliation and interest-group influence being more important in the House than the Senate (Mariott 2005).

This suggests that members' voting preferences on a morality-type issue generally reflect the choice position of the denomination or faith with which a member is affiliated. Since partisanship is not perfectly correlated with religious affiliation, this suggests that both Republicans and Democrats of the same faith have a tendency to vote similarly despite pressure from their respective parties (Mariott 2005).

Mariott also reported that "the effect of religious affiliation on choice votes for the Senate showed mixed results. In the 106th Congress it was significant, while in the last two years studied it did not show a significant effect on choice votes. This confirms my earlier hypothesis that religious affiliation matters less to a senator on choice votes than to a member of the House" (2005). He suggested that the difference in length of terms makes it possible for senators to be held less accountable than House members for their votes on morality issues. His findings led him to conclude that morality issues do not fit the typical voting model, where lobbyists are more in control. Instead, lobbyists play only minor roles on morality issues, whereas in matters such as military budgets and taxes, lobbyists are more influential in determining the outcome (2005). Mariott seems to downplay religious lobbyists such as the United States Conference of Catholic Bishops, as well as many Evangelical, Jewish, and Mainline Protestant lobbying groups.

Interest in the religious factor in the U.S. Congress continued to grow and expand. Other examples include James Guth's "Religion and Roll Calls: Religious Influences on the U.S. House of Representatives, 1997–2002" (2007); "Is Religion a One-Trick Pony? An Empirical Study of the Impact of Religious Affiliation on Voting in Congress," by Nate Wheatley (2010); "Substantive Religious Representation in the U.S. Senate: Voting Alignment with the Family Research Council," by Lauren E. Smith, Laura R. Olson, and Jeffrey A. Fine (2010); and *Religion and American Politics: Classic and Contemporary Perspectives*, edited by Amy Black, Douglas Koopman, and Larycia A. Hawkins (2010).

Guth identified three types of religious groupings—belonging, behaving, and believing—and used them to analyze roll call votes in the House for the period 1997–2002. He also used a modified version of James Davison Hunter's 1991 culture wars hypothesis by adding a centrist group to the fundamentalist and progressive extremes (Guth 2007).

Wheatley (2010) explored a series of issues other than abortion, such as the Brady bill, the North American Free Trade Agreement (NAFTA), and the death penalty, and found support by religious affiliation to be inconsistent. Smith et al. (2010) found support for the hypothesis that senators' personal religious affiliations—along with the religious makeup of their constituencies—affects the extent to which they voted in line with the Family Research Council.

Finally, the book edited by Black et al. (2010) provided historical and contemporary perspectives on religion and American politics from more than one hundred writers, including one chapter on religion and Congress.

Our study provides a forty-year view of voting patterns in the House and Senate. Based on the pioneering work of Benson and Williams (1982) and the research cited above, we expect religion to play an important role in at least some of the issues coming before Congress in the period 1969–2010.[3] The Supreme Court's decision in *Roe v. Wade* in January 1973, which made abortion legal at the national level, was supported and opposed by secular and religious groups, with strong opposition from Catholic laity groups and bishops and many Mormon and Evangelical leaders. Benson and Williams (1982) made us aware of the Evangelicals' arrival on the national scene, with abortion being one of their main concerns. Our analysis of roll call votes beginning in 1969–1970 enables comparisons before *Roe v. Wade* and the emergence of Evangelicals in Congress.

Our study differs also in that we began with a strong interest in public opinion polling on the wide range of issues that came before Congress in the 1970s and 1980s. The public opinion surveys focused primarily on the tendency of the American people to cluster near the center on most issues. Abortion was the one issue that revealed polarizing differences between people who strongly identified with one or the other political party. The irony of this finding was that during most of the time since *Roe v. Wade* (1973), a majority of Americans believed that abortion should be legal in all or most cases, although there was volatility in the 1980s and 1990s as those groups opposing abortion found ways to apply restrictions.

This is shown graphically in figure 1.1 (Jones et al. 2011). At the time of their research in May 2011, Jones et al. reported that "nearly 3 in 10 (29%) Americans said abortion is a critical issue facing the country today; an equal number (29%) said that it is one among many important issues; and 4 in 10 said it is not that important compared to other issues" (Jones et al. 2011, 6).

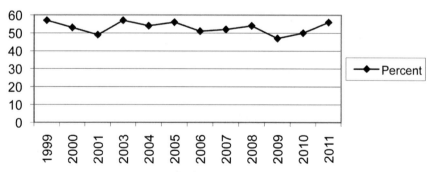

Percentage of Americans who say abortion should be legal in all/most cases

Figure 1.1. Views on Abortion, 1999–2011
Source: Pew Research Center

Studies consistently showed a majority of Catholics, Mainline Protestants, and Jews supporting abortion rights in some or all cases (DiMaggio, Evans, and Bryson 1996; Evans, Bryson, and DiMaggio 2001; Evans 2002a, 2002b; Gitlin 1995; Hall and Lindholm 1999; Hunter 1991, 1994; Luker 1984; Mouw and Sobel 2001; Smelser and Alexander 1999; Williams 1997; Wuthnow 1988). The only religious group opposed to abortion all or most of the time was Evangelicals.

A THEORETICAL FRAMEWORK[4]

The framers of the Constitution, particularly James Madison, were well aware of the power of religion to split a nation apart. In recent years the wisdom of our founding fathers has been challenged as the Republican Party has identified itself with the political agenda of Christian conservatives. . . . Throughout my time in the Senate, abortion was an issue on which Republicans did not agree. By and large, religion was not a political subject in those years.

—John Danforth (2006, 4, 6)

Much scholarly attention has been devoted to the polarization resulting from the culture wars that presumably wracked American society during the latter part of the twentieth century and into the early years of the twenty-first century. According to proponents of the culture wars thesis, conflict over such politicized social and moral issues as abortion, homosexuality, affirmative action, and school prayer had become so divisive and intractable that compromise between factions was rendered difficult, if not impossible, to achieve. As groups lacking the common ground necessary for compromise staked out increasingly polar positions, the stability of the two-party political system was threatened—or so the argument went.

What was at the core of this conflict? Hunter argued that the divisions caused by issues like abortion reflected opposing ideological visions of the "good society." On the one hand, the good society was seen as grounded in an orthodox, transcendent understanding of the world, based on God-ordained fundamental beliefs, values, and norms. People simply have to obey the laws God has given them, found in books like the Bible, where God's words are to be understood literally and accepted as inerrant (Hunter 1991, 1994).

On the other hand, a progressive view of the good society sees life as unfolding and truth to be sought through science and reason. This view does not necessarily deny the existence of God so much as it affirms the capacity of human beings to create their own moral codes based on reason and lived experience as well as scripture, tradition, and history. This view has its roots in the Enlightenment and the rise of science in the seventeenth and eighteenth centuries and also manifests a continuing tension between reason, science, and religious faith.

The culture wars thesis has been both challenged and affirmed. In the mid-to-late 1990s, critics pointed to the substantial body of public opinion data from the previous quarter century, which showed little, if any, increase in attitudinal polarization along the lines found in Hunter's models.[5] DiMaggio, Evans, and Bryson found little evidence of increased polarization in public opinion during the period 1971–1996, with one important exception: when controlling for political party identification of respondents, they found that abortion attitudes deviated dramatically between self-identified Republicans and Democrats (1996, 735–36).[6] Reflecting on the implications of these party divisions, DiMaggio et al. stated, "In traditional pluralist theory, social conflict emerges from struggles between groups in civil society. Political parties, seeking support from the vital center, take the rough edges off of such conflicts." They went on to conclude, "Our findings—that the social attitudes of groups in civil society have converged at the same time that attitudes of party identifiers have polarized—raise troubling questions about the role of political parties in a pluralistic society" (738).[7] Their concern—expressed some sixteen years ago at a time when the forces in Congress that led to the polarization we now confront were just beginning to form—has been confirmed, as we now find public opinion as much driven by the kinds of Congress the electorate has voted into office in the past sixteen years as by their own extreme views. In Danforth's words,

> Christian conservatives believe that God's will can be reduced to a political program, and that they have done so. In their own minds, there is indeed a Christian agenda for America, and in recent years, they have succeeded in pressing it upon the Republican Party. It is an agenda composed of wedge issues which, when hammered relentlessly in political forums, divide the American people. (2006, 55)

In this book, we address the issue of culture wars and polarization by focusing not only on public opinion polls but also on the voting patterns of those elected to Congress. It is in those voting patterns that we expect to show the growing asymmetry between the parties, leading to the dysfunctionality reported by Mann and Ornstein (2012). In the process, we show how the religious factor, often a variable that helped bring about compromises across party lines, has been trumped by the asymmetry delineated by Mann and Ornstein in their book. We begin with its most celebrated exemplar: abortion. Americans who are drawn to the fundamentalist, orthodox vision of the good society have developed an anti-abortion position that became anchored in the Republican Party in the 1980s and has greatly increased its dominance there since.[8] Evangelicals, Mormons, and a wide variety of Catholic groups—both lay and clerical—support this position. On the other side, NARAL Pro-Choice America (formerly the National Abortion and Reproductive Rights Action League) and other pro-choice groups—including Mainline Protestant denominations, Jewish groups, secularists, and Catholics for Choice—view abortion as a woman's right to choose in some, most, or all situations, as spelled out in the 1973 *Roe v. Wade* decision.

Since 1980, the abortion issue has become more than just a difference of belief or opinion. Rather, it has become an anchoring point for two distinct visions of what the good society is about. Beyond abortion, these visions of the good society are manifested in the ways the two parties differ on taxes, small versus big government, helping the poor, housing, raising the minimum wage, and an assortment of social programs that fundamentalist conservatives see as futile, socialistic, or even immoral and that progressives insist are in keeping with promoting the general welfare.

It is instructive to understand the two visions as they were originally portrayed by Hunter, as end points on a continuum (1991). Real human beings share varying degrees of the beliefs and values embedded in the two visions. As shown in a wide range of polls, not everyone who is strongly anti-abortion is necessarily a believer in the inerrancy of the Bible. Nor are pro-choice supporters necessarily secular humanists who deny the possibility of a creator God. We understand the asymmetry between the two parties, as described by Mann and Ornstein, to mean that Republicans are closer to the fundamentalist/conservative end point than Democrats are to their progressive end point. In fact, Mann and Ornstein assert that "this asymmetry between the parties . . . constitutes a huge obstacle to effective governance" (2012, 103).

CLERICS' VISIONS OF THE GOOD SOCIETY

Putnam and Campbell (2010) provide a number of vignettes showing the distinctive ways American clergy link religion and politics. A good example of the fundamentalist vision is provided in their interview with Reverend Raymond "Mac" Hammond. Mac and his wife Lynne formed their own church, Living Word Christian Center, in 1980 in Minneapolis, and it has grown to become the largest church in Minnesota. With little formal training for the ministry, Rev. Hammond affirmed his right to lead because he "is grounded in the Word to know," he explained. "Early on I felt that the Lord had pressed me that the one thing that always had to be in place was clear, concise, in-depth teaching of the Word as it relates to the principles of people's daily lives" (323). Further on, he explained that "we are not a denomination, we are an evangelical, Spirit-filled church" (325). To new members he explained, "I am the one who is responsible. I am anointed to do this. I'm called to set the direction of the ministry" (326). He continued to explain his position in these words:

> I do not believe . . . that there is, at least in our founding documents, an intent for church and state to be separated in the way that it has been perceived by our courts in the last fifty years. . . . I am saying this: There are people whose views are more closely aligned with the values we hold dear than other people. . . . OK now, as we've pointed out, you vote in line with the Word, and what it has to say among the basic issues of morality. . . . The right to life is one of the most basic of moral issues, and the government should *not* be legislating against these morals. . . . Now we're not going to politicize this process in the church. (326, 330)

Hammond then reminded the congregants of the two-page "non-partisan" voter guides that had been distributed, which compared Obama and McCain on twelve key issues in the 2008 campaign. He concluded by distinguishing between the key social issues—welfare, immigration, free trade, and foreign policy—and moral issues, which are "things spoken to by the Ten Commandments," saying, "Forget the social issues! Your vote is in line with the moral issues!" (331).

Putnam and Campbell noted that the members of Living Word are "thrilled" with Pastor Mac and "appreciate a preacher who doesn't apologize for the fact that . . . 'the Bible says what it means and means what it says'" (2010, 334). In this regard, Rev. Hammond insisted that "God wants you to be a winner in every aspect of life" (326). Thus, in a 2006 sermon he preached, "you can never have too much money" (326). The church's magazine, *Winner's Way*, expounds on "[b]iblical principles that will enhance your spiritual growth and help you to win at work, win in relationships, and win in the financial arena" (326). Another example of this vision of God is provided by Joel Osteen, the senior pastor of the Houston-based nondenominational Lakewood Church. He preaches a positive message of self-help Christianity without alluding to the conservative values that underpin Hammond's preaching. Osteen's father founded the Evangelical church, having been a former Southern Baptist minister. As a megachurch, Lakewood Church is the largest congregation in the United States, averaging more than 43,500 in attendance each week.[9]

At the other end of the political/religious spectrum, Putnam and Campbell took us to a Saturday morning service at Beth Emet, The Free Synagogue, the largest Jewish Reform congregation in the Skokie-Evanston, Illinois, area. It claimed a membership of 840, with about 10 percent active in one or another aspect of synagogue life. A key feature of the synagogue was its free pulpit. Free pulpit meant that "the rabbi was free to have his opinions and to speak what he wanted to say. And that went for anybody else in the synagogue too" (2010, 341). Rabbi Knobel taught that "for Reform Jews, the autonomy of the individual was central, as was the idea that ethics should be imposed by one's own reasoning rather than by tradition" (342). Rabbi London shared her congregants' focus on *doing* rather than *believing*: "As we say about Judaism, we're a religion of deed, not creed" (344). Their activism ranged from marching in Selma with Martin Luther King Jr. to opening the first soup kitchen in Evanston. One of the congregants put it this way: "Being a member of Beth Emet has allowed me to live out my sense of Jewish identity by working on social justice issues with talented and committed people" (346).

Putnam and Campbell's study of Living Word Christian Center and Beth Emet are real-life examples of the two visions of the good society that Hunter had delineated some twenty years earlier.[10]

Our objective is to ascertain whether and to what extent the polarization found by DiMaggio et al. only with regard to attitudes toward abortion among those citizens with strong political party identity (1996)—and now delineated by Jones et al. (2011) regarding the opinions of white Protestants and white Catholics in the period from 1972 to 2010—is reflected in the roll call votes of House and Senate members on key issues during the last thirty years of the twentieth century and first part of the twenty-first century. In the process, we hope to gain new insight on the role of religion within and between parties. But even if there is significant polarization in both public opinion and in congressional voting, are the public and Congress doing anything more than what our Constitution encourages, as Meacham states in the quotation that opened this chapter?

CONFLICT, COMPROMISE, CONSENSUS: DEMOCRACY?

S. M. Lipset addressed the issue of polarization and summarized it in an essay on moralism, social movements, and violence in American politics: "All complex societies are characterized by a high degree of internal tension and conflict, but consensual institutions and values are necessary conditions for their persistence. Hence, any effort to deal with political or social systems must treat conflict and consensus" (Lipset 1985, 1). Lipset's arguments provide context for the present study. Though conflict, violence, and polarization may be threats to the consensus necessary to maintain a stable, effective democratic system, they are, as Lipset noted, "as American as cherry pie"; yet their intensity "makes difficult the kind of compromise which has sustained the two-party system" (315).

Has ideological conflict within the halls of the U.S. Congress challenged the two-party system and raised new concerns about the ability of our political system to function in the face of growing polarization? Ours is a pluralistic democracy, built on a Constitution that has distributed power so as to create a system of checks and balances. Can such a democracy become seriously polarized by the infusion of religious beliefs and values that have proven to be divisive and polarizing, threatening the uneasy balance and compromise that are seen to be essential to maintaining some degree of balance? That was the question facing us as we wrote this book.

Mann and Ornstein (2012), in their new book *It's Even Worse Than It Looks*, blame the Republican Party for the dysfunctional Congress. Their findings on what has happened in and to the U.S. Congress since their 2006 book *The Broken Branch* led them to abandon their role as academics always looking for ways to provide a balanced review of congressional politics. In their words:

> The dysfunction that arises from the incompatibility of the U.S. constitutional system with parliamentary-type parties is compounded by the asymmetric polarization of those parties. Today's Republican Party, as we noted at the beginning of the book, is an insurgent outlier. It has become ideologically extreme; contemptuous of the inherited social and economic policy regime; scornful of compromise; unpersuaded by conventional understanding of facts, evidence, and science; and dismissive of the legitimacy of its political opposition, all but declaring war on the government. The Democratic Party, while no paragon of civic virtue, is more ideologically centered and diverse, protective of the government's role as it developed over the course of the last century, open to incremental changes in policy fashioned through bargaining with the Republicans, and less disposed to or adept at take-no-prisoners conflict between the parties. This asymmetry between the parties, which journalists and scholars often brush aside or whitewash in a quest for "balance," constitutes a huge obstacle to effective governance. (Mann and Ornstein 2012, 103)

We should note that Mann and Ornstein do not address religion as a factor in the current turmoil. Religion is only mentioned in passing once on page 52 and it is referred to as part of the Christian Right.

In sum, our examination of roll call votes on all major issues between 1969 and 2010 enables us to add another dimension to the public opinion surveys that portended the decline of the center in public opinion and the gradual rise in conflict and polarization in public opinion and in the halls of Congress—and now showing itself in what Mann and Ornstein (2012) call the asymmetrical dysfunctionality of the Republican Party.

E. J. Dionne argues similarly in his new book *Our Divided Political Heart* (2012) that disagreement over the proper role of government is central to our polarized politics:

> [Our] country has witnessed the rise of a radical form of individualism that simultaneously denigrates the role of government and the importance most Americans attach to the quest for community. Critics see both as antithetical to the strivings of free individuals who ought to be as unencumbered as possible by civic duties and social obligations. This extreme individualism sees the "common good" not as a worthy objective but as a manipulative slogan disguising a lust for power by government bureaucrats and the ideological ambitions of left-wing utopians. This view has transformed both American conservatism and the Republican Party. (5–6)

A BRIEF OVERVIEW OF THE CHAPTERS AHEAD

Chapter 2 presents a brief historical overview of the major religions brought to these shores by the English, the Spaniards, the French, and a variety of European countries, beginning in the sixteenth century and continuing now into the twenty-first century with new religions from other continents. The chapter gives special attention to the Mainline Protestant denominations that dominated society through the colonial period and into the first century and a half of its independence. Their cultural values, beliefs, and practices created a Protestant ethic that continues to resonate. The chapter also brings to life the conservative, now even fundamentalist, Evangelical Protestantism that has kept alive the belief in the United States as "The City on a Hill," an inerrant Bible, and suspicion about science, especially evolution. Into this mix came the Roman Catholic Church, varieties of Judaism, and a wide range of smaller sects.

Chapter 3 addresses the question of how, if at all, the various religious denominations and sects were and are reflected in the religious makeup of the U.S. House and Senate. There is a brief look at the First Congress and its religious makeup and how different it looks from the present makeup. Here we focus on the ways the House and Senate have or have not changed over the period 1959–2010. The once-dominant Protestant denominations have gradually ceded their places to Catholics, Jews, and black Protestants. In the process, we compare the religious makeup of the two parties and note the relationship between religion, political party, and region of the country. We note how the waves of European immigrants have become visible within the two parties in both houses and discuss the growing presence of the more recent immigrants in the halls of Congress.

Chapter 4 examines all roll call votes on abortion beginning in 1977–1978 and concluding with the 110th Congress's vote on the health care bill. It shows how in the early years, roll call votes were not determined by party alone and how that changed over time. Thus, we examine abortion not as a conflict of beliefs and opinions among the populace at large but as a divisive political issue involving the votes of members of Congress. Is the polarization among the public reflected also in Congress, as suggested by Evans? Has it become so because the two parties have increasingly taken on polarizing positions? DiMaggio et al. pointed out that increases in disagreement are important because they "militate against social and political stability by reducing the probability of group formation at the center of the opinion distribution and by increasing the likelihood of the formation of groups with distinctive, irreconcilable policy preferences" (1996, 693).

Chapter 5 presents an in-depth analysis of three key issues found in roll call votes over the four decades of our study. The key vote areas are defense spending, welfare spending, and taxes. These were selected from a total of seventeen sets of key votes derived from Michael Barone's book series *The Almanac of American Politics* (1972–2010).

In chapter 6, Steven A. Tuch and Alyx Mark employ Poole's Common Space NOMINATE scores to explore whether abortion and the other key issues examined in previous chapters are uniquely polarizing or, rather, exemplars of a more general pattern of increasing ideological polarization in Congress.

Chapter 7 provides an analysis by Robert Jones and Dan Cox of public opinion polls (1972–2010) that show how white Protestants and Catholics became polarized in their attitudes toward abortion and same-sex relationships beginning in the Reagan administration and increasing, in both cases, into the second decade of the twenty-first century.

Chapter 8 summarizes our key findings, relates the voting patterns to the two distinctive visions of the good society, and concludes that the ideologies of both political parties are rooted in religion.

2

Religion in Congress

A Historical Overview

An examination of the religious affiliations of U.S. senators and representatives shows that, on one very basic level, Congress looks much like the rest of the country.

—David Masci and Tracy Miller (2008)

When it comes to the question of religion, of the ways in which we understand God and ourselves and what that relationship means, when it comes to the question of our commitment to our religious beliefs and the way in which we live them out, there is very little difference between the members of Congress and the rest of us. We elect them from among us.

—Peter L. Benson and Dorothy L. Williams (1982)

Among the three branches of government, Congress is said to be the one that most reflects the broader populace. Whether the statement was or is accurate broadly regarding race, ethnicity, and social class, our focus in this chapter is on the religious beliefs and values of the House and Senate members over the past fifty years. Our question is this: To what extent has the religious composition of the U.S. House and Senate reflected the religious makeup of the U.S. population during this time period? That raises two other questions: What difference does it make whether Congress does or does not reflect the religious makeup of the United States? How, if at all, were religious beliefs and values translated into legislation during those four decades? In the following chapters, we will attempt to answer these questions.

We expect that members of Congress, much like the rest of America, hold a wide range of personal religious beliefs and values, and if they are like the general American population, they may question the relevance of some or all of them, especially as they might affect legislation. As Benson and Williams (1982) noted, very little serious scholarly work has focused on the role of religion in the halls of Congress throughout most of its history. By the mid-twentieth century, social scientists had accepted the theory of a rationalizing, secularizing world in which religion had been reduced to a matter of personal piety (Casanova 1994). So it is not surprising to discover that there is little written material about it. Slowly at first, and now with a more certain step, scholars are probing the impact of religion as a factor in congressional decision-making. We know from research cited in chapter 1 and almost daily experience in recent years that religion has played a role in congressional decision-making (Hertzke 1988; Guth 2007; Mariott 2005).

In this chapter, we sketch out the major beliefs, values, and attitudes of the Protestant denominations that helped shape the ethos which dominated American social and political life from the eighteenth century well into the twentieth century. We also examine how Catholics and Jews who were part of the "great white migration" from Europe to America during the period 1870–1925 adapted to the Protestant ethos as they found their own way into this society. We begin with a brief historical overview of the religious groups that have been present in Congress from the earliest years. This helps provide the context for our broader goal: probing the influence, growth, and impact of religion in Congress as seen in members' roll call voting patterns within the period 1969–2010.

HISTORICAL OVERVIEW

Looking back to the first American Congress (1787–1788) provides some perspective on the shifts that have occurred over the last two centuries. The Episcopalian, Congregational, and Presbyterian churches—with smaller numbers belonging to Christian Reformed, Catholic, and Quaker denominations—were the religions the 66 members of the First Congress acknowledged. What is a more interesting statistic about the first House was the number and percentage of members who gave no religious affiliation: 20 out of that 66, or nearly 30 percent. Today, it is extraordinary to think that one-third of the members of the 1st House did not report a religious affiliation. In the 111th U.S. Congress (2009–2010), 5 Democrats (1 percent of the House) provided no affiliation. In the 1st Senate (1787–1788), 5 of the 30 members (17 percent) gave no religious affiliation; again Episcopalians dominated, with 13 members (45 percent). The 5 who gave no affiliation were the second-largest grouping in the 1st Senate. In the 111th Senate, no one reported "no affiliation," while 7 percent said only that they were Protestants. In the 113th

Congress, for the first time a newly elected representative said she was a "non-believer." It has been a matter of conventional wisdom that to be elected to national office one had to identify with a religious group or denomination. That the times may be changing is suggested by recent polls showing that one out of five American adults now say they have no religious affiliation.

The United States in the mid- to late eighteenth century was grappling with its sense of national identity. The relationship between religion and politics in colonial America was colored by the dominant ideas of the day, many stemming from principles of the Enlightenment (perhaps reflecting the high percentage who reported no religious affiliation). There was also a strong element of Puritanism in the colonies (Benson and Williams 1982, 86). Both the Enlightenment and Puritanism contributed to Americans' ideas about shaping the new republic. Still, the unique fabric of early American society was woven around what Benson and Williams referred to as a "nation-building religion," because the perspective of so many Americans in this period was based on the influence of Puritanism.[1] Presbyterians, who traced their reform movement to John Calvin via the Scotsman John Knox, had arrived in Philadelphia in 1706 and quickly became influential in religious and state affairs.

Puritans, or Congregationalists, rebelled against the ideal of a centralized religious authority. Rejecting the pope and the king of England, Puritans sought to organize their religious governance at the local or congregational level. Each congregation operated independently from the others in the way that they felt mirrored the congregational independence of the early Christian church. By 1740, Presbyterians—who were also more like Congregationalists in their method of organizing their churches—had settled in Maryland, Virginia, and the frontier areas where the Anglican Church had not made its presence felt. These early American Protestants played an active role in the First Great Awakening with their focus on making the Bible easy to understand and on hearty hymn singing. The Great Awakening in the nineteenth century was aided by the advances in printing press technology and the construction of the railroad and other infrastructure projects such as the Erie Canal, which created access to the new settlers and made the mass production of Bibles affordable for even the poorest farmers. Its impact was felt across the existing Protestant denominations and from it emerged new Christian-based movements such as the Seventh-Day Adventists, the Church of Christ, Methodists, Jehovah's Witnesses, and Mormons.

Drawing inspiration from the Bible that the New World was a "Promised Land," the Puritans and Pilgrims created their colonies with the belief that God had a special plan for developing America (Benson and Williams 1982, 89–93). This mentality that God had a special role for the United States became widely accepted by other denominations. The phrase "God Bless

America," which presidents and other politicians frequently invoke when trying to unify the country, is a reflection of the widespread acceptance or perception of God's special role for America. Thus, from the founding of the republic, God was perceived either as standoffish after endowing "man" with the intellect to organize society or as the active engineer of a great American design.

Those who believed the latter felt united in their belief that the ideals of freedom, hard work, prosperity, and promise would lead them toward a national destiny in keeping with divine intent. According to Benson and Williams, "It was a world view that bound the nation together, cutting through the theological and cultural divisions of the day" (1982, 93). Indeed, though not all citizens of the early American republic agreed, the idea of a providential God with a divine plan for the new nation served as a guiding and sometimes unifying force for a vast number of Americans during this period. Hertzke (1988, 23–26) pointed out that from Jonathan Edwards on, church leaders were actively engaged in trying to influence government policies.

MAINLINE PROTESTANTISM (LIBERAL AND MODERATE)

This study identifies Mainline Protestant churches as composed of two groups: the theologically "liberal" denominations (Episcopalian, Presbyterian, and Congregationalist/United Church of Christ) and the more "moderate" denominations (Methodist, Lutheran, Northern Baptist, Disciples of Christ, and Christian Reformed). The Episcopal Church, drawn from the Anglican tradition, advocated a relationship between religious and civil life that was best exemplified by the practices of the Church of England. Under this model, "the church and state cooperate . . . to promote good governance and sound religion, but the state reign(s) supreme, even on issues of doctrine and clerical leadership" (Anderson 2009, 93). As the Anglican tradition blended into Liberal Protestant churches, American independence reflected the uneasy relationship between religion and the state, which, in turn, affected the founding of the American nation. In particular, the passage of the First Amendment to the U.S. Constitution made clear that a separation must exist between the government and religions (101). American Protestantism has maintained the Anglican tradition of high respect for the state and citizen participation in politics, but only within the context of separately operating church and state functions. Indeed, much of the purpose of a constitutional separation of state and church was to avoid the institutional replication of the Church of England in the United States, which was the primary reason why the Puritans, Pilgrims, and many Presbyterians left England. Thus, the

Liberal Protestant tradition has been largely credited with shaping the cultural and social, in addition to political, realms of American life (Demerath 1995).

The typical mind-set of Liberal Protestantism has largely depended on a distinction between religious and civil life. A question that arises is how recent membership changes in the Protestant denominations have affected this mind-set.[2] Though it is difficult to discern definitively what drives believers toward or away from particular churches, it is undeniable that the Liberal and Moderate Protestant denominations in recent years have experienced a sharp decline in membership and an even sharper decline in church attendance. The decline is especially apparent when controlling for generations, as is also true for Catholics and for Mainline Protestants and Jews (D'Antonio et al. 2007, 39–43; Jones and Cox 2012; Putnam and Campbell 2010, 70–71, 74–80). Nevertheless, the principles espoused by Liberal Protestantism seem to have interjected themselves into most American religions (Smith and Snell 2009). This is especially true of the value placed on personal autonomy, that is, that each of us is responsible for our own behavior and that means we owe allegiance to our conscience. Yet, as Jonathan Edwards noted in the eighteenth century—and de Tocqueville wrote about in the nineteenth century—personal autonomy, correctly understood, meant that we were at the same time individuals as well as responsible members of our family and our local community. This interplay between the individual and the social continues to challenge, divide, and unite us in our religious and civic lives. And they have been no guarantee of support for the denominations that anchored them. Columnist Joseph Bottum noted the decline in membership of Liberal as well as Moderate Protestant churches:

> Over the past thirty years, Mainline Protestantism has crumbled at the base, as its ordinary congregants slip away to evangelicalism, on one side, or disbelief, on the other. But it has weakened at the head, too, as its most serious theologians increasingly seek community—the longed-for intellectual culture of people who speak the same vocabulary, understand the same concepts, and study the same texts—in other, stricter denominations. (Bottum 2008, Section IV)

Arguing that the decline in Mainline Protestantism has negatively affected American culture, Bottum described Mainline Protestants' positive contributions in earlier American history:

> Protestantism . . . gave America something vital: a social unity and cultural definition that did not derive entirely from political arrangements and economic relations. And America gave Protestantism something in return: a chance to flourish without state interference, a freedom to fulfill the human desire for what lies beyond the material world. (2008, Section VII)

With little of this mind-set remaining in modern America, the separation of church and state that was so vital to Mainline Protestants has become a weakened notion in contemporary American political culture. And within Christianity, the beliefs, values, and moral precepts of Conservative Protestant and Catholic groups seem to have more forcefully entered the fold. Still, while Mainline denominations have suffered significant losses in membership, they continue to be overrepresented in the House and Senate, reflecting the educational and other social capital they continue to bring to American political life.

CONSERVATIVE PROTESTANTISM

The ideological foundation of Conservative Protestantism was based on the rejection of the Enlightenment. During the period from the 1920s until the late 1970s, the dominant Evangelical stance was to stay clear of politics. Evangelicals gave Jimmy Carter, a Southern Baptist, their support but were soon disillusioned with his presidency. When Reagan reached out to the Evangelicals led by Jerry Falwell in 1980, the tide changed. They not only backed Reagan but also obtained key positions within important party committees. As a result, for most Conservative Protestant groups now, the church tends to play a slightly more integrated role in the state, largely because they see the state as the means to promote their ends, especially to promote their vision of the good society, centered in a very conservative sexual morality, as spelled out in chapter 1. History—or the lack of a history—also plays a critical role as to why Conservative Protestants are less wary of church and state integration.

These Christian churches emerged many years after the colonization process and beyond the American Revolution. In the minds of many Conservative Protestants, the church and state are "separate and unequal, with an elevation of church over the state" (Joireman 2009, 77). The most important role for government is to maintain peace and stability so that the church can operate effectively. The main groups identified under the Conservative Protestant heading are Southern Baptists and other Evangelicals/Fundamentalists, such as Nazarenes, Pentecostals/Holiness, Assemblies of God, Church of God, Adventists, and (included here primarily due to their conservative voting patterns) Mormons. For the majority of these Conservative Protestant groups, the state is understood to be an important factor in the moral and spiritual formation of individuals because it provides the order necessary for such moral and spiritual foundations to flourish.

Like most groups placed together in a similar category, Conservative Protestants are by no means universal in their positions on the proper role of the state. Various groups under the Conservative Protestant heading can—and do—have differing perspectives on the degree to which religion and politics should be involved. Groups such as the Anabaptists hold a more extreme position on the role of the state, viewing it as little more than a tool for maintaining order. In this belief, separation of religion and government is necessary for the church to fully perform its work. Sandra Joireman explained the Anabaptists' position: "Order created by the state allows the church to grow and the gospel to be spread" (Joireman 2009, 77). Other groups under the Conservative Protestant umbrella view the state's role as more expansive, believing it to be capable of both providing order and supporting moral growth. In other words, although separation of church and state is key, the state still can possess a positive spiritual function. President George W. Bush's administration had an Office on Faith-Based Initiatives, which exemplified this perspective.

Timothy Samuel Shah described modern-day Evangelicals as generally skewing toward this depiction. Explaining the development of this perspective, he noted:

> On the one hand, Evangelicals generally favored a sharply limited political role for themselves, as well as a sharply limited political role for the state. On the other hand, Evangelicals believed that the state was an appropriate and necessary instrument for the redress of moral and social evils they perceived to be significant. (2009, 124)

Thus, by this view, the political sphere provides an arena for airing concerns about issues related to the moral well-being of society. For many Conservative Protestants, this kind of justification led to political activism that was motivated primarily by spiritual or moral concerns of the church (Campbell 2007).

ROMAN CATHOLICISM

Catholic influence in the United States has increased steadily over the years. A group that comprised only a small fraction of the American population in the eighteenth century has emerged in modern society as a dominant power in terms of both membership and political involvement.

Spanish (in Florida and the then-Mexican Southwest) and French (parts of New England and later Louisiana) Catholics were among the early settlers of the colonies; the most significant Catholic colony (one of the English Catholics) was located in Maryland. The first great Catholic migrations began in the 1830s with Germans, followed in the 1840s and 1850s by the Irish. Then, from 1870 to 1925, the United States experienced the great white migration from all parts of Europe. This migration also brought with it millions of Protestants, especially Lutherans, as well as additions to the other Mainline Protestant churches. It also included millions of Jews as well as Irish, Italian, and Polish Catholics. Their presence was felt especially on the East Coast and in the Midwest in cities undergoing rapid industrialization.

Immigrants filled the factories, shops, and coal mines and worked the railroads. Catholic priests and bishops built the Catholic Church and ministered to the growing numbers of new citizens. One of the most sensitive problem areas was exacerbated by an expanding public school system. While the final step in the formal separation of church and state had occurred in Massachusetts in the 1840s, the reality was that the public school system throughout the country was imbued with

> a "common core" of religious education based on Protestant teachings and ethics as well as a curriculum intended to inculcate students into the practice of "American" traditions, which were often greatly influenced by Protestant, Anglo-Saxon traditions. This led to resentment and resistance on the part of Catholic laity and Church leadership alike. (Froehle and Gautier 2000, 64–65)

Church leaders were determined that education should not include "Protestantizing" the growing waves of Catholic immigrants. The bishops held a series of plenary councils, culminating in the Third Plenary Council held in Baltimore in November 1884. The seventy-one bishops present mandated the establishment of a Catholic school in every parish, with pastors and parishioners responsible for funding the schools and all parents required to send their children to these parochial schools. Over time, ethnic parishes built their own Catholic schools, thus not only ensuring the passing on of the faith but also retaining core aspects of their community's culture and language, at least for another generation. This had the further effect of building the ethnic factor into the two-party political system because it helped to solidify American Catholics as a political constituency. The Catholic school system continued to increase in its influence and reached its peak in the 1960s, with almost half the Catholic student population enrolled in some thirteen thousand Catholic schools (Shah 2009, 68).

Politically, Catholic involvement has found a strong foothold through the lobbying efforts of Catholic bishops as well as individual church members. The United States Conference of Catholic Bishops (USCCB), in particular, has had a significant role in promoting public policies that reflect the church's teachings. Professing to "promote the greater good which the church offers humankind," the USCCB draws upon the Catholic Church's overall aims of benefiting the common good and general welfare of society. The Catholic Church as a whole does not see itself as operating separately from the state but rather—especially since Vatican Council II in the 1960s—in connection with it. Viewing the state as both a necessary and formative part of culture and society, the Catholic Church finds the state to be a useful means for realizing its primary aim, promoting the common good (Shelledy 2009, 17).

Robert Shelledy describes the Catholic perspective as being based on a social understanding of humanity—that is, people and their relationships withone another are at the forefront of Catholic social teaching (2009, 18). Thus, the Catholic perspective on government and the state is a natural extension of this understanding. The state has a responsibility not just to safeguard its citizens but also to positively influence their conduct. More recently, the Catholic Church has sought to realize this principle through the standards outlined in the Second Vatican Council (1962–1965) and the resulting publication of *Gaudium et Spes*, both of which were designed to illuminate the Catholic Church's position in the modern world and, in particular, in the political realm (22). As a result of these examinations, "the church moved toward a tolerance of pluralism and the promotion of religious freedom," and its ideological position became more clearly defined as one in which efforts by the state and society, regardless of whether they are explicitly Catholic in nature, will be supported by the Catholic Church as long as they foster the common good (22).

In recent decades, American Conservative and Libertarian Catholics such as Reid Buckley and Paul Ryan (R-WI) have adopted the principle of subsidiarity, which is a Catholic social teaching that postulates that government should only manage those initiatives that exceed the ability of individuals or private sector groups' independent efforts. Pope Leo XIII first formally developed the principle of subsidiarity in the 1891 encyclical *Rerum Novarum* as a means to formulate a compromise between laissez-faire capitalism and various forms of communism, which sought to subject the individual to the state. Subsidiarity, as defined by American Conservative and Libertarian Catholics, is fundamentally opposed to increased centralized or federal governmental efforts. Government functions are believed to be best handled at the local level whenever possible. Republican Catholics such as Speaker of the House John Boehner (R-OH) and Representative Paul Ryan adhere to this approach, which helps to justify their reluctance to increase federal government social spending.[3]

Most bishops continue to insist that the social teachings from Leo XIII to the present pope involve the interplay of subsidiarity with solidarity, the latter grounded in the belief that the state has a moral responsibility to provide for the needs of the poor when individuals and groups at the local level are not able to do so. These needs include health, housing, clothing, and a living wage. Catholics in the Democratic Party like Minority Speaker Nancy Pelosi

(D-CA) and Rosa DeLauro (D-CT) have been strongly committed to these two principles.

In recent years, there has been a growing gap between the bishops and the Catholic laity not only on the social teachings on subsidiarity and solidarity but also on a wide range of issues involving human sexuality. Catholics look increasingly to their own consciences rather than to Church teachings on matters ranging from contraception to same-sex marriage. The sex abuse scandal and cover-up efforts by some bishops have further increased tensions since 2002 (D'Antonio et al. 2007, 2013).

JUDAISM

Jewish influence on American culture, following a pattern similar to Catholic political influence, has substantially grown during the period of this study (1959–2010). However, Judaism faces a different situation than Catholicism in terms of its ability to prescribe and maintain a unified set of principles to its believers. Catholicism's long tradition of hierarchical communications, combined with a committed core of adherents, gives the Catholic message unparalleled reception and sustainability in America (Wald and Martinez 2001, 378–79). Judaism, while possessing a strong religious tradition, lacks the hierarchical structure of Catholicism, and its doctrine is often subject to a variety of interpretations, which is seen by many Jews as one of its strengths.

Political scientists Kenneth Wald and Michael Martinez described the increasing range of interpretation in Judaism as a consequence of the course of Jewish history. They noted that "the diversity within Judaism is a function of religious development as abetted by Diaspora," and they pointed to "revivalist and reformist protests" within Judaism over the last few centuries as key factors within this process (Wald and Martinez 2001, 379). Readers should not misconstrue the varying streams of Judaism as described here: This depiction does not imply that the core principles of Jewish faith have been devalued in any way, but rather it shows that the diversity of movements within Judaism has allowed it to adapt to a plethora of societies, cultures, and communities. In the United States, this attribute essentially gives Jews the opportunity to establish political standpoints that are relative not to any finite set of global principles but to their distinct American environment and experiences.

The Jewish position in the United States is indeed unique.[4] Paul Burstein points out that Jews as a group "are much more successful educationally and economically than other ethnic, racial, and religious groups in the United States" (Burstein 2007, 209). The explanations for this disproportionate success (in relation to the number of members of other religious groups) range from human capital models, in which, just as for non-Jews, education and a strong work ethic are seen as the driving factors of increased wealth, to particularity models that ascribe Jewish success to traditional Jewish values and lifestyle, including mutual aid societies where Jews offer assistance to one another (214). Regardless of why Jews in America tend to be more economically successful than other Americans, this attribute has become an interesting factor in the study of Jews and their role in American politics.

In terms of political involvement, Jews have largely identified with the Democratic Party since the era of FDR (Greenberg and Wald 2001, 163).[5] In Congress, this partisan attachment to the Democratic Party is even more pronounced: "As a minority that has thrived in a multicultural state that disclaims a formal religious identity, American Jewry has developed a distinctive liberal political culture" (381). The Jewish religion, very much a part of Jewish culture, is grounded in passages like Deuteronomy 26:5–11, in which Hebrews, pilgrims themselves, learn to reach out to strangers and aliens in their midst, and Genesis 18:1–15, where we learn of Abraham's encounter with three strangers in the heat of day, whom he welcomes to his tent, provides water for washing, and has his wife Sarah provide a feast, thus confirming God's teaching that "thou shalt not turn thy back on the stranger [foreigner]."[6] Prophets and other writers follow suit down through the ages, stressing the responsibility to reach out to the needy: "To whom much is given, much will be required" is a phrase much used by Jewish and Christian political leaders. Senator Joseph Lieberman, when he first appeared on television and radio after Senator Al Gore selected him to be the vice presidential running mate on the Democratic ticket in 2000, used this phrase to help explain his political values and beliefs. The Jewish understanding of who they are makes for a liberalism that sees government as having a responsibility to act to promote the general welfare. Thus, though there is space for a range of opinions within Judaism, most Jews tend to have a more liberal perspective overall. As this translates into the relationship between religion and the political sphere, the liberal viewpoint is more heavily weighted toward the separation of church and state.

SUMMARY

Protestant beliefs, values, and attitudes dominated American society and continue to influence people of other religions and ethnicities, even as Mainline Protestantism itself with its own social gospel teachings, continues to gradually lose members, political influence, and social sway. Whereas the early

American view of God was an amalgam of varied beliefs but was tied intrinsically to the nation's prosperity and growth in the contemporary era, the nation's view of God today is divided. On the one hand, God has become tied to the prosperity and growth of the individual who lives by the laws God has ordained. That individual believes God's teachings in the Bible are without error, including the belief held by almost one-third of all Americans that God created the world in seven days, about six thousand years ago (Benson and Williams 1982, 94). This return to religious fundamentalism is increasingly a one-party experience, with its focus on a limited set of moral values and financial frugality. On the other hand, the religious beliefs of the other party reflect a broad concern for the common good. These contrasting beliefs have polarized dissent and made compromise unreachable. Conflicting beliefs have led to conflicting views on the proper role of church and state relations.

In broad terms, this chapter explored how Mainline Protestant, Conservative Protestant, Catholic, and Jewish groups have established themselves in contemporary America, particularly with respect to their positions on church and state relations. Thus, party ideologies are rooted in their religious beliefs, which are shared less and less across parties. Knowing if a person is a Catholic or a Methodist says little about their political ideology without identifying their political party (Hertzke 1988, 78–79).

The November 2010 elections brought a dramatic change to the U.S. House: Catholic Republicans increased their numbers from 39 to 63 while Catholic Democrats saw their numbers drop from 94 to 69; Protestant Republicans won 164 seats compared with 84 won by Democrats. Overall, Republicans won 242 seats (up from 179), while Democrats won only 193 (down from 256). Democrats retained control of the Senate (53 to 47), with 22 Protestants, 15 Catholics, 12 Jews, 2 Mormons, and 2 "other." Among Republicans were 34 Protestants, 9 Catholics, 3 Mormons, and 1 "other."

CONCLUSION

American religious groups have been shaped by a variety of religious traditions, both old and new. Many religious groups have flourished in America since the nation's earliest years, but only a small number have made their way into the halls of Congress. How much and in what ways do religious denominations affect the operation of politics in modern America? What is the relationship among party ideology, the religious makeup of the two parties, and congressional voting? These are the questions we will examine in the following chapters.

3

Religious Composition of the U.S.
House and Senate, 1959–2010

Chapter 2 presented an overview of the beliefs, values, and attitudes of the religious groups that have dominated the U.S. Congress for more than two centuries. Chapter 3 focuses on the changing nature of the religious composition of Congress in the years since 1959. Most of the changes are found not in an increased number of religious denominations with which members identify; rather, the eighteen different religious groups noted among senators in 1959 declined in number to fifteen in the 2010 Senate.[1] The most significant shifts have been among and within a relatively small number of existing religious groups and within and across party lines.

To introduce this discussion of the religious composition in Congress, we begin with a description of the denominations that are or have been represented. Figure 3.1 shows the current percentage of the population that is identified with each of these denominations.

The United States is now and always has been a country dominated by a variety of Protestant churches descended from the Protestant Reformation of the sixteenth and seventeenth centuries. However, the percentage of Americans who identify as Protestant has decreased from 74 in 1960 to 50 percent in 2010. The Mainline Protestant churches (Liberal and Moderate in figure 3.1) now report a membership total of some 54 million (18 percent of adult Americans), having lost more than 20 percent of their members. The Conservative Protestant churches have grown, with between 26 percent and 28 percent of the total (including Southern Baptists, the Church of God in Christ, the Assemblies of God, and a host of other Evangelicals and Fundamentalists). Because of their similar voting patterns, we will include the Church of Latter-Day Saints (Mormons) with the Conservative Protestants. Though American Jews now have about the same percentage (2 percent) of the popu-

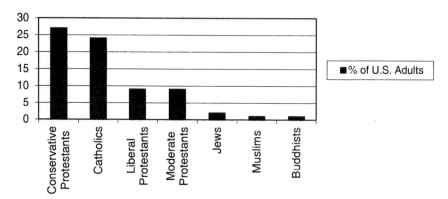

Figure 3.1. Percent of U.S. Population Identified with Each Religious Denomination
Sources: Pew Forum, 2008; "Religion in the United States, National Council of Churches Yearbook," February 2011; Hartford Institute for Religion Research, 2011.[2]

lation as the Church of Latter-Day Saints, Jewish representation in the House and Senate lead us to include them in our analysis.

In the first decade of the twenty-first century, one in four adult Americans self-identified as Roman Catholics, making them the single largest religious group. Meanwhile, some 20 percent of Americans said they had no religious affiliation (a mixture of agnostics, atheists, and unaffiliated believers). The historic black churches reported a membership of 7 percent (21 million) but were included in figure 3.1 under several categories. We now turn to the question: To what extent did the members of the House and Senate reflect this changing American religious environment?

CHANGES IN THE NUMBER AND DIVERSITY
OF RELIGIOUS GROUPS IN THE U.S. HOUSE

This section charts changes in the religious affiliations of House members over the past fifty years. The important changes were found not so much in the addition to or disappearance of religions over time; rather, it was in the growth or decline in numbers of members identifying with different religions both within and across the two political parties. Figure 3.2 shows the changes in the membership of major religious groups that occurred in the House since the 86th Congress (1959–1960).

In figure 3.2, we combined the Liberal and Moderate Protestant denominations into the single category Mainline Protestants.[3]

As indicated in figure 3.2, in 1959 more than half of House members (57 percent) identified with the Mainline Protestant churches. By 2010, their

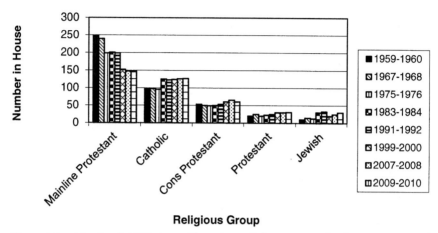

Figure 3.2. Members' Affiliation with Major Religious Groups in the U.S. House of Representatives, 1959–2010

members had lost more than one hundred seats, while Roman Catholics increased their numbers by more than a third (from 90 to 133). Thus, Mainline Protestants, with 34 percent of House seats, and Roman Catholics, with 31 percent, held about two-thirds of all House seats. Conservative Protestants experienced a modest amount of growth in the House as well, holding about 78 seats (18 percent) in 2010, up from 60 seats (14 percent) in 1960. Some of this growth came from the increase in the number of African American Baptists in Congress, largely a consequence of the Civil Rights Act (1964) and the Voting Rights Act (1965).

In addition to the increase in Catholics in the House, those members who identified themselves as Protestant or Christian are identified in the table as Protestant; they doubled in number over fifty years from about 20 (5 percent) to 37 (9 percent) in 2010. While congressional composition has changed, the general population has also changed, but in a different direction. For example, according to the Pew Forum, one in five Americans now have no religious affiliation. Jewish members have more than tripled their numbers in the House since 1959, when they constituted only 2 percent (9 members) of the total. By 2010 they constituted 7 percent (30 members). The House then had two Muslim members and one Buddhist member, all Democrats.

A comparison of the makeup of the religious population of the United States (as seen in figure 3.1) with the makeup of the U.S. House shows that Catholics were the single largest denomination in the nation, constituting 24 percent of the total. They comprised 31 percent of the House, where they were overrepresented. Mainline Protestants, who held 34 percent of House seats, had a total national population of about 18 percent and thus were even more overrepresented than Catholics. Conservative Protestants (including Fundamentalists, Pentecostals, Evangelicals, and Mormons)[4] constituted 28 percent of the population, yet they held only 18 percent of seats in the House. It is also the case that some members who identified as Methodists, Presbyterians, or Lutherans might well be born-again Christian Evangelicals, especially if they were located in the South.

In the following pages, we look at the changes that have taken place in the House beginning with a breakdown of Mainline churches into more specific denominations. These are the denominations that have most significantly shaped the culture and institutions of American society.

As previously indicated, Liberal and Moderate Protestant denominations have experienced a downward trend with both groups' numbers declining substantially since the 86th Congress. Moderate Protestants, who comprised 26 percent of the total House in 1959, held only 18 percent of House seats in 2010. Liberal Protestants experienced a more marked decrease in membership, holding 31 percent of the House in 1959 (the largest religious group at the time) but only 15 percent of the House membership in 2010. House Members who described themselves as simply "Protestant" or "Christian" almost doubled in numbers from 5 percent in 1959 to 9 percent of the House in 2010.

Major Conservative Protestant groups in the House include Baptists, evangelical groups, and Mormons. Baptists have increased in numbers by about 20 percent, largely due to the growing presence of African Americans in Congress. Though Baptists experienced a decline in membership entering the 94th Congress (1975), their numbers steadily increased subsequently and leveled off in the 111th Congress (2009–2010), with their adherents comprising about 13 percent of the total membership of the House.[5] In addition to the Southern Baptists, other Evangelicals and Mormons grew in membership overall; although neither held a sizable percentage of the House between 1959 and 2010, their numbers have roughly doubled in both cases (non-Baptist Evangelicals from three to six House members, and Mormons from four to nine).

RELIGION AND PARTY AFFILIATION—U.S. HOUSE

When reviewing the patterns of religious affiliation that characterize the two parties in the House, several questions arise: Do the two parties attract members more or less randomly from the array of religious groups in the population? Or does their political ideology influence the probability that candidates will be nominated by one or the other party? Which religious groups, regard-

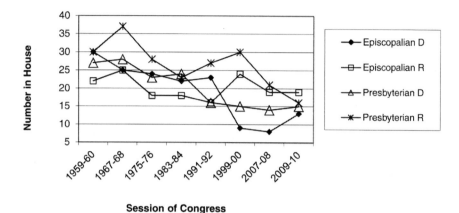

Session of Congress

Figure 3.3.   Number of Episcopalians and Presbyterians (by Party) in the U.S. House, 1959–2010

less of their size in the general population, have tended to dominate either one or both parties in the House? Were these changes in the size of the specific religious groups within each of the parties? Figures 3.3, 3.4, and 3.5 display most of the major Mainline Protestant denominations—subdivided by political party—and their membership trends between 1959 and 2010.[6]

In 1959, there were more Episcopalian Democrats than Republicans in the House. Over time, the number of Episcopalian Republicans held more or less steady around twenty, while the number of Episcopalian Democrats declined from twenty-nine to thirteen. A somewhat similar pattern of decline is seen among Presbyterian Democrats, whose numbers declined from twenty-eight to fifteen. The number of Presbyterian Republicans varied more widely, but

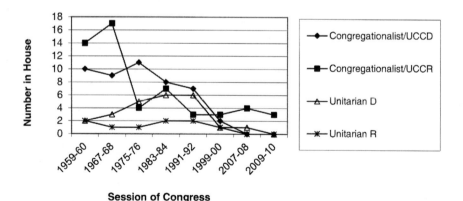

Session of Congress

Figure 3.4.   Congregationalists and Unitarians in the U.S. House (by Party), 1959–2010

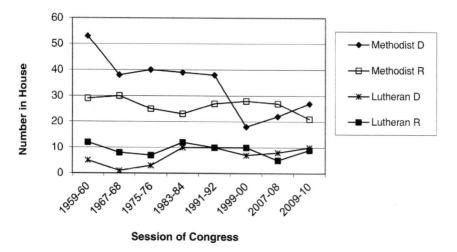

Figure 3.5.   Methodists and Lutherans in the U.S. House (by Party), 1959–2010

again by 2010, with the election of the 111th Congress, their number was only slightly larger than that of their Presbyterian Democratic colleagues, and smaller than the Episcopalian Republicans.

Congregationalists (now United Church of Christ) and to a lesser extent the Unitarians were significant in the formation of the New England culture and social system, and in the early years of the House. Yet, in the last fifty years, they have practically disappeared from the House. Both denominations currently have national population totals under 1 million each.

Throughout this fifty-year period, there were always more Methodists than Lutherans in the House, although the gap between them has closed. Through most of this period, Methodist Democrats outnumbered their Republican co-religionists. Meanwhile, the Republican advantage among the Lutherans has disappeared. Over the past several elections, Lutherans have averaged about twenty House seats each time. Methodists, with about 8 million adherents nationally (under 3 percent), have averaged about fifty seats in recent elections. There is not much difference in the pattern among Disciples of Christ and Reformed Christians in the House.

As shown in figures 3.3, 3.4, and 3.5, there is some evidence of party difference when it comes to membership in each of the various Mainline Protestant denominations; the overall decrease in numbers for most Mainline denominations is not always proportionate to party affiliation. Among Episcopalians in the House, for instance, Democrats experienced a much steeper decline in numbers than did Republicans. Methodist Democrats in the House also lost more members than their Republican counterparts did. Democratic Lutherans, however, represented one of the few Mainline Protestant subsets

that experienced an increase in membership over the years. For Congregationalists and Unitarians, party differences did not seem to have a discernible (or at least a lasting) effect on the overall membership. For most of the
smaller groups (not shown), it is difficult to track the relationships between
their representation in the party and their share of the overall population.

Factoring in party affiliation when looking at the Conservative Protestant
groups leads to some sharper divergences. Figure 3.6 shows how party divisions have affected membership in the Baptist denomination in the House
since 1959.

The great majority of Baptists in Congress in 1959 were white Democrats;
today, African American representatives constitute a growing minority of
Baptists in Congress. The changing composition of the South and its racial
diversification have affected the composition of Congress as well as the party
divisions among Baptists. In recent elections, Baptists have averaged about
13 percent of the House; they constitute 17 percent of the population.

Evangelicals other than Southern Baptists in the House have generally
been overwhelmingly Republican. But they have always been small in
number, varying from one in the 86th Congress (1959) to a high of ten in
the 110th (2007); in the 111th there were five.[7] There were two Evangelical
Democrats in the 86th Congress. Since then, they have struggled to keep a
presence, with only one in the 111th. Also in the 86th Congress there were
two Mormon Republicans in the House. Over the years, the number of Mormons rose to as many as ten in the 106th Congress (1999–2000); in 2010
there were seven. The number of Democratic Mormons has varied from two
in the 86th to five in the 102nd (1991–1992) and back to two in the 111th. In

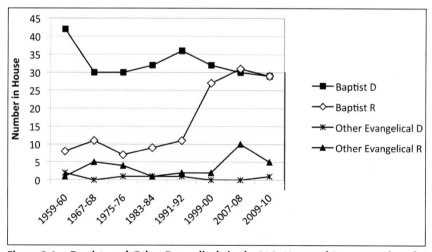

Figure 3.6.   Baptists and Other Evangelicals in the U.S. House of Representatives (by Party), 1959–2010

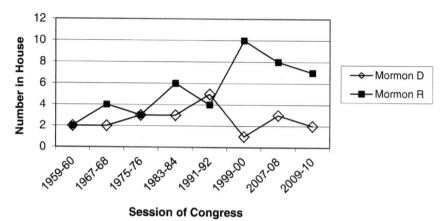

Figure 3.7.   Mormons in the U.S. House of Representatives (by Party), 1959–2010

the last several elections, Mormons have been averaging about nine members, with Republicans holding a three-to-one advantage.

All of the major Conservative Protestant groups in the House increased in overall membership between 1959 and 2010, owing largely to greater Republican numbers.

Trends among Catholic and Jewish members in the House also followed party lines. Figure 3.8 shows the growth of both religious groups in the House and how this has translated across party lines.

As shown in figure 3.8, throughout most of the period from 1959 to 2010, Catholic and Jewish Democrats greatly outnumbered their Republican co-

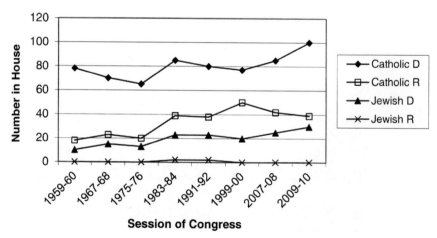

Figure 3.8.   Catholics and Jews in the U.S. House of Representatives (by Party), 1959–2010

religionists in the House. Catholic Republicans also increased in number, while the number of Jewish Republicans never exceeded two.

SUMMARY OVERVIEW: THE HOUSE

Of the major religious groups, the starkest party-line differences tended to appear among those that have gained House membership over the last half century (Conservative Protestants, Catholics, and Jews). In the groups that lost membership over the years (primarily Mainline Protestants), party differences tended to be less pronounced.

CHANGES IN THE NUMBER AND
DIVERSITY OF RELIGIOUS GROUPS: SENATE

Some similar patterns occurred in the Senate as in the House between 1959 and 2010. Mainline Protestants generally lost seats over time, whereas the number of Catholic and Jewish members grew significantly. Jewish members gained Senate seats by a substantial percentage, holding thirteen seats in 2010 after holding only two seats in 1959. Catholics, who held twelve of the Senate seats in 1959, more than doubled their numbers to twenty-six in 2010. Conservative Protestants in the Senate saw their numbers slightly decline after 1959 and generally level off during the 102nd (1991–1992) to 111th (2009–2010) sessions of Congress.

Liberal Protestants (including both parties) experienced substantial gains in the Senate from 1959 to 1992, achieving a high of thirty-eight Senate seats in the 102nd Congress. Since then, their numbers declined to twenty-two seats of the Senate in 2010. Moderate Protestants had a slightly steadier decline in Senate membership, going from twenty-seven seats in 1959 to sixteen in 2010. Senators identifying as simply Protestant or Christian gained slightly, going from four in 1959 to seven in 2010. Again, Mainline Protestants were greatly overrepresented in Congress during this fifty-year period. In 2010, Mainline Protestants still held thirty-eight seats, while their total numbers in the population had declined to some 18 percent.

Baptists are the largest Conservative Protestant group in the Senate (primarily Southern Baptists), followed by Mormons, whose numbers ranged between three and five. Between 1959 and 2010, Baptists generally lost members, from fourteen to eight seats. Mormons did not vary greatly in their numbers over the years, typically holding between three and five seats. Other Evangelical groups never gained significant numbers in the Senate but remained consistent, not holding more than two seats at any given time.

It is interesting that although Evangelicals constitute about 28 percent of the adult population, between 70 percent and 80 percent vote Republican. They also appear to be significantly underrepresented in Congress during the past fifty years. Part of this apparent underrepresentation is found in the reality that some of the Mainline Protestants may well be born-again Evangelicals. In order to gain some idea of the extent to which senators who identify themselves as Mainline Protestant church members may well be Evangelicals—or at least among Southern Conservatives—we decided to compare Mainline Protestant Republicans who were in the Senate in 1969 with those in the Senate in 2010. In 1969, only nine of the forty-one Republican Protestant senators were from Southern states. In this same year, thirty-two identified as being members of Mainline churches. In 2010, twenty-two of the thirty-seven Republican Protestant senators identified as members of Mainline churches, and all but nine of them were from Southern states. As with President George W. Bush, at least some are born-again Mainline Christians, thus partially explaining why Evangelicals appear to be underrepresented.

CHANGES IN PARTY AFFILIATION IN THE SENATE

We now look at party affiliation in the study of religious groups in the Senate. Figures 3.9 through 3.13 show the Mainline Protestant denominations, subdivided by party, and their membership trends between 1959 and 2010. Although other Mainline Protestant groups held membership in the Senate over the years, their numbers were minimal—usually not more than one seat at any given time. Therefore, only groups with larger numbers have been included here.

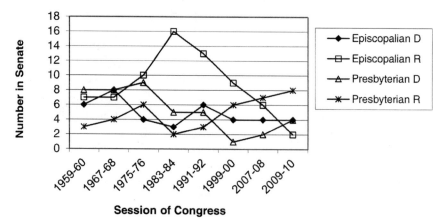

Figure 3.9.   Episcopalians and Presbyterians in the U.S. Senate (by Party), 1959–2010

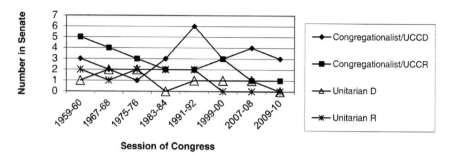

Figure 3.10. **Congregationalists (UCC) and Unitarians in the U.S. Senate (by Party),** **1959–2010**

As shown in figures 3.9 through 3.11, some Mainline Protestant groups were affected by party divisions more than others. Among Episcopalians in the Senate, both Democrats and Republicans declined in numbers after 1959. The Republican decline has been more dramatic, from a high of sixteen seats in the Senate in the 98th Congress (1983–1984) to only two seats in the 111th Congress (2009–2010). Presbyterian Democrats lost half their seats between 1959 and 2010, while Presbyterian Republicans more than doubled their numbers over the same period.

UCC/Congregationalist Democrats gained a few Senate members in the 102nd Congress (1991–1992) but then declined to only three Senate seats in 2010 (the same as in 1959). Congregationalist Republicans declined from five to only one Senate seat, while Unitarians of both parties never held more than two Senate seats since 1959. By 2010 Unitarians had completely disappeared from the Senate. Methodist Democratic and Republican senators have also declined in representation since 1959, though Methodist Demo-

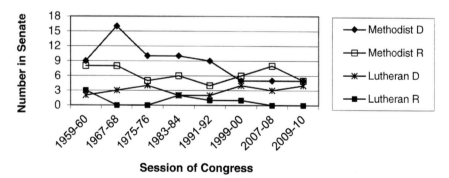

Figure 3.11. **Methodists and Lutherans in the U.S. Senate (by Party), 1959–2010**

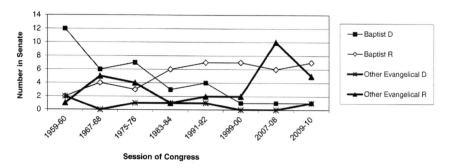

Figure 3.12. Baptists and Other Evangelicals in the U.S. Senate (by Party), 1959–2010

crats initially gained substantial members heading into the 90th Congress (1967–1968) before declining. Lutheran Republicans, though holding three Senate seats in 1959, had no representation by 2010; Lutheran Democrats, conversely, increased their Senate membership, doubling their numbers from two seats in 1959 to four by 2010.

Figures 3.12 and 3.13 show how party divisions affected membership in the major Conservative Protestant denominations in the Senate between 1959 and 2010.

Among both Baptists and Mormons in the Senate most growth occurred in the Republican Party. Democratic numbers decreased among Baptists as more Southern white Democrats became Republicans. The number of Mormons increased marginally in recent sessions, although they were not underrepresented. Among other Evangelical groups, it was difficult to discern any trend (along party lines or otherwise) given the very low Senate membership of these denominations (other than Southern Baptists). Again, the fact that such a significant proportion of Republican senators since the 1980s personally identified themselves as Evangelicals while they were still formally affiliated with Mainline churches most likely means that the number of Evangelicals in the Senate was undercounted.

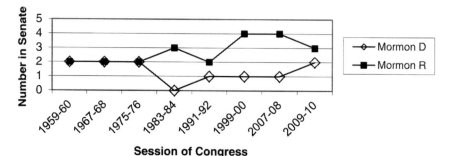

Figure 3.13. Mormons in the U.S. Senate (by Party), 1959–2010

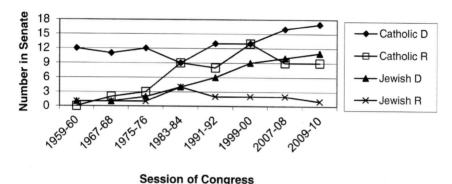

Session of Congress

Figure 3.14. Catholic and Jewish members of the U.S. Senate (by Party), 1959–2010

Catholics and Jews increased their numbers in the Senate between 1959 and 2010. Figure 3.14 indicates that Catholic Republicans twice matched Catholic Democrats in number (in 1983 and 1999, with Democrats again leading fifteen to nine in 2009–2010), so it would seem that both parties have experienced a substantial increase in Catholic representation. Jewish Democrats increased in number from one to eleven, while Jewish Republicans in the Senate nearly vanished, declining from four seats in the 98th Congress (1983–1984) to only one seat by 2010.

SUMMARY

In the Senate, the number of Mainline Protestants declined significantly after 1959. After holding sixty-four in the 90th Congress (1967–1968), Mainline Protestants continued to decrease (to a low of thirty-eight seats in 2010). However, they continued to be overrepresented (constituting only 18 percent of the population in 2010). Catholic and Jewish senators increased, with Catholics holding twelve Senate seats in the 86th Congress (1959–1960), increasing to twenty-six seats in 2010—about equal to their percentage of the national population. Jewish senators also sharply increased, going from two to thirteen Senate seats over the fifty-year period. During this time, the Jewish percentage of the population dropped from 5 percent to 2 percent. The decline of Mainline Protestants in the Senate was matched by the increase of Catholics and Jews, constituting a dramatic shift of representation in the Senate. This shift also occurred in the House at almost the same time. Catholics, in particular, grew from a modest presence in 1959 to becoming the largest single religious group in Congress by 2010. In the process, the numbers of Catholic Republicans in Congress increased unevenly, but by 2010 they were also a significant part of the Republican caucus. A similar pattern had not yet appeared among Jews, who were overwhelmingly Democratic by 2010 (for a fuller explanation, see Wald's commentary in chapter 2, as well as the Jones-Cox survey of American Jews and their values in chapters 1 and 2 in this volume).

CONTEMPORARY POLITICAL-RELIGIOUS ISSUES

Many social factors contributed to the ever-changing composition of the U.S. Congress. What remained consistent was the significance that Congress members and the American public alike attributed to religion and party affiliation. What this descriptive recount does not do is provide evidence about the awareness American voters may have had regarding the religious affiliation of those who ran for public office. Did voters base their decisions on the religious or political beliefs of their candidates? How did parties select their candidates? For example, in 2006 Democratic leaders supported Robert Casey to run against a fellow (but very conservative) Catholic, Republican senator Rick Santorum. Both were pro-life but differed greatly regarding Catholic social teachings. Senator Casey won easily.

Next, we turn our attention to the role that the changing religious composition of Congress may have played in key roll call votes during the period of 1969–2010. We begin with abortion. In 2009, Congress faced the daunting task of reforming the current American health care system. Health care legislation proved to be a divisive issue in both the House and Senate. As the debate on health care grew, so too did the religious implications of health care reform. Abortion, in particular, became a critical issue in framing the debate, as certain provisions of proposed health care legislation came under fire for perceived infractions on either side of the abortion issue.

Chapter 4 addresses the unique role that the issue of abortion played in American politics between 1973 and 2010, including the battle over health care reform. The chapter examines how abortion—perhaps more than any other issue—has moved to the forefront of the American political-religious scene in the time since the 1973 *Roe v. Wade* decision.

4

Abortion

Exemplar of the Polarized Congress?

When we began our study of religion in Congress, abortion was one of a variety of issues that might account for a growing polarization in Congress, if not in the public itself. Over time, disagreement grew between those who call themselves pro-life because they claim an embryo is sacred from the moment of conception and those who call themselves pro-choice because they support a woman's right to choose an abortion. At the national level, there is little place for dialogue between these two positions, and polarization is now at a high point in both houses of Congress. The "culture wars," cited by Hunter in 1991, seem to be a reality acknowledged by the media, political leaders, and scholars.

On one side are Catholic bishops, related Catholic organizations, and Evangelical Protestant and Mormon leaders who insist that a child exists from the moment of conception; on the other side are Mainline Protestant churches and Jewish groups, Catholics for Choice, and Republicans for Choice ("Pro-choice Republicanism" 2011). The abortion controversy has affected the acceptance of the Affordable Care Act.[1] It has generated controversy and political upheaval that will impact American politics for years to come.

How did this come about? What explains the politicization and polarization of abortion issue votes? What role did the presidential elections of 1976, 1980, and later have on the polarization process? What clues might we find from an examination of House and Senate roll call votes between 1977 and 2010?

BACKGROUND

This chapter examines the issue of abortion not only as a conflict of opinion within the populace at large but also as a political issue involving congressional voting. Below we review the public's support for, or opposition to, abortion as well as the role it has played in presidential politics.

ROE V. WADE

In January 1973, the Supreme Court ruled to support a woman's right to abortion by a vote of seven to two. In the years that followed, anti-abortion groups (identified as pro-life) began to lobby for restrictions on abortion, including eliminating funding of abortion (e.g., for pregnant women in the military and government and for Medicaid and other government programs). The Hyde amendment was passed in 1976 and barred the use of certain federal funds to pay for abortions. It is not a permanent law but a "rider" that has been attached to annual appropriation bills since 1976. It primarily affects Medicaid[2] and has become the mechanism by which pro-life groups have been able to prevent federal funds from supporting abortions. Nevertheless, this amendment *does* allow for exceptions in the case of rape or incest or to save the life of the mother.

During the years following *Roe v. Wade*, a strong majority of Americans supported the right to abortion in some or most situations. Only a small minority (less than 20 percent) opposed the right to an abortion under any circumstance. Recent polls (Gallup and Pew Forum 2009–2010) showed the nation more evenly split on the issue.[3]

Party positions and alignments on abortion rights were unclear, especially at the presidential level, until the 1980 presidential election. That year, a strong anti-abortion plank became part of the Republican platform while the Democrats took a mildly pro-choice position. In a provocative and controversial essay titled "Criss-Cross: Democrats, Republicans, and Abortion" (2006), George McKenna presented a compelling argument on why the Democrats should have been the pro-life party and the Republicans the pro-choice party, based on their contrasting ideologies at that time. The core values of the Democratic Party were, in his words, "highly congenial to Catholic social teaching." He continued, "The Democratic Party and the Catholic Church have always been on the same wave length as regards social and economic rights, particularly the rights of the poor, weak, and vulnerable members of society" (63).

McKenna saw the Republican Party as the Protestant party, with its roots in Puritanism and later in Mainline Protestantism. In the 1960s and 1970s,

Republican leaders such as Rockefeller, Reagan, and George H. W. Bush were abortion rights supporters, and Mainline Protestant churches were more neutral on the abortion issue. On the other side, Jimmy Carter was known to oppose abortion, and a number of Catholic senators, including Ted Kennedy and Joe Biden, were leaning pro-life. The bishops failed to convince Carter to support a constitutional amendment to reverse *Roe v. Wade*, while Gerald Ford, the Republican incumbent in 1976, accepted a moderate plank in the Republican platform for a constitutional amendment that would respect life.

The failure of the bishops in 1976 to convince either party to adopt a platform plank to overthrow *Roe v. Wade* left them on the sidelines in the 1980 campaign. Meanwhile, Reagan successfully courted the Evangelicals, led by Rev. Jerry Falwell. Charles B. Moore, at that time the executive director of the Family Life Seminars, provided a fascinating account of how he worked with a well-known conservative Catholic priest, Fr. Don Shea, to arrange a meeting of Evangelical leaders and Republican Party leaders, at which time the Evangelicals agreed to support the Republican Party.

During the time between the *Roe* decision and the 1980 election, Catholic bishops, the Christian Right, Southern Baptists, and other conservative and Evangelical groups as well as leaders of the Mormon Church took strong stands against abortion. Pro-choice and pro-life groups became major lobbying forces in the halls of Congress, while both political parties gradually hardened their positions on abortion. By 1984, the abortion issue had become political dogma, with Republicans under Ronald Reagan being ardently pro-life and Democrats increasingly pro-choice. The selection of a pro-choice Catholic, Geraldine Ferraro, to join Walter Mondale on the Democratic ticket in 1984 only served to heighten the partisan divisions on this issue.

In a 1984 speech at Notre Dame University, then New York governor Mario Cuomo enunciated a position that attempted to reconcile Catholic beliefs with public responsibilities. Cuomo's speech became a kind of political doctrine for elected Democratic Catholic leaders. In it, he defended his view that Catholics can and should participate in public life, while also giving their highest priority to their oaths of office—not to religious dogma—when it came to faithfully executing public laws:

> The Catholic who holds political office in a pluralistic democracy—who is elected to serve Jews and Muslims, atheists and Protestants, as well as Catholics—bears special responsibility. He or she undertakes to help create conditions under which all can live with a maximum of dignity and with a reasonable degree of freedom; where everyone who chooses may hold beliefs different from specifically Catholic ones—sometimes contradictory to them, where the laws protect people's right to divorce, to take birth control, and even to choose abortion. In fact, Catholic public officials take an oath to preserve the

Constitution that guarantees this freedom. And they do so gladly. Not because they love what others do with their freedom, but because they realize that in guaranteeing freedom for all, they guarantee our right to be Catholics: our right to pray, to use the sacraments, to refuse birth control devices, to reject abortion, not to divorce and remarry, even if we believe it to be wrong. (Cuomo 1984)

During the 1990s, candidates from both major parties tried to soften the differences on the abortion issue. In 1992, Bill Clinton's refrain was that abortions should be "safe, legal, and rare." Bob Dole disliked the harsh language of the 1996 GOP platform on the abortion issue, arguing instead for a line in the platform that would read, "We recognize the members of our own party have deeply held convictions and sometimes differing views on issues of personal conscience" (White 2003, 87). Dole believed that his party could hardly reject the insertion of a plan Ronald Reagan himself had once approved as governor of California. However, Ralph Reed, the executive director of the Christian Coalition, threatened to withdraw his support for the Republican ticket unless its presidential and vice presidential candidates opposed abortion. Pro-life supporters maintained that abortion could not be "tolerated" (88). GOP platform chairman and ardent pro-life activist Henry Hyde threatened to quit his position on the committee. Dole acknowledged defeat, as his effort to soften the party's stance on abortion was rejected by Republican delegates, who handed him a stinging rebuke on the eve of his party's nomination. Fed up, Dole claimed he did not have time to read the platform and that, in any event, he did not feel honor-bound by it (88).

The choice of Ferraro in 1984 and Kerry in 2004 highlighted a movement among a small number of Catholic bishops seeking to warn Catholic politicians that they risked being denounced by church leaders and priests if they opposed the Church's stance on abortion. When Ferraro attacked Reagan on religious grounds—observing that he was "un-Christian" because his policies were so unfair to the poor and needy—she became the target of many Catholic prelates who took her to task for what they took to be her positions (White 1988, 20). Similarly, many Catholic prelates took John Kerry to task for his pro-choice views in 2004. That year, Catholic prelates in several cities (Camden, New Jersey; St. Louis, Missouri; Lincoln, Nebraska; Denver, Colorado; and Colorado Springs, Colorado) issued statements forbidding Kerry from receiving Holy Communion should he attend mass in their dioceses (Dowd 2004). The Colorado Springs bishop, Michael Sheridan, went further, noting that Catholics who supported Kerry were jeopardizing their salvation by supporting any candidate who backed abortion rights (Wakin 2004). Charles Chaput, at that time the Denver archbishop, described Catholic voters for Kerry as "cooperating in evil" (Dowd 2004).

In the 2008 national campaign, both candidates and parties tried to find their voice on the abortion issue. McCain and Palin claimed the anti-abortion mantle, but Obama gained a significant debate victory when in response to a question about his being pro-abortion, he responded that "no one is pro-abortion" (Second Presidential Debate, September 5, 2008). With his electoral victory, pro-choice advocates were hopeful that he would take executive actions that would undo some of the strong pro-life actions of former president George W. Bush. Obama's insistence on getting a major national health care bill passed took an extraordinary effort and cost much in national support for both Obama and the Democratic Party. Ultimately, it undermined any effort to loosen restrictions on abortions, as we shall see shortly.

In an article published in 1999, Michael Hout analyzed a variety of demographic, religious, and political variables in an effort to understand how a single-issue social movement—in this case, abortion—became a mainstream political movement. He concluded the following:

1. The abortion debate brings Americans' disagreements about sexual morality and women's rights into the political spotlight.
2. The major demographic groups differ on abortion pretty much according to how they differ about sexual behavior and women's roles.
3. In the years immediately following the *Roe v. Wade* (1973) decision, the disagreements were not politically organized. Liberals and conservatives were internally divided over the issue.
4. During the 1980s, "conservatives coalesced around a pro-life agenda and liberals coalesced around the issue of protecting the abortion rights that followed from the *Roe* decision." What could not be determined from the analysis was whether "the polarization has arisen because people who had made up their minds on abortion changed their political identity accordingly or whether people with a fixed political identity came to adopt the abortion stance that is 'correct' for their political position" (28).

We now turn to the way the House and Senate responded to *Roe v. Wade* as expressed in a series of roll call votes beginning in the period just after the 1976 elections and ending with the passage of the Patient Protection and Affordable Care Act on March 21, 2010.

THE FINDINGS

Our primary source of data on abortion-related voting in Congress is NARAL Pro-Choice America (formerly the National Abortion and Reproduction Rights Action League [NARAL]). NARAL provided information on roll call votes on abortion for all members of the House and Senate. Since NARAL's lists did not identify members of Congress by political party or religion, we used Barone's *Almanac of American Politics* and other sources for information and confirmation on party and religious affiliation of all members of Congress from 1977 to 2010.[4]

In chapter 3 we demonstrated that Catholics increased moderately in number within both parties in the House and Senate, while the number of Jews grew dramatically; the same was true for black Protestants. On the other hand, the number of Mainline Protestants decreased in both parties, while Conservative Protestants increased in numbers, especially within the Republican Party. Since these changes occurred during the period that *Roe v. Wade* became law, they may have affected the roll call voting on abortion bills. Mainline Protestant denominations have a moderate pro-choice position on abortion; most Jewish groups have a pro-choice position that gives priority to the woman; most black churches are theologically opposed to abortion; the Catholic position is opposed to abortion in any and all conditions; and Evangelicals, Mormons, and other conservative churches are all strongly opposed to abortion, although some allow for choice in cases of pregnancy due to rape or incest or to save the life of the mother.

Regarding abortion, the larger picture was that party affiliation eventually trumped religion, except for a significant minority of Catholic House Democrats who consistently cast pro-life votes. At the same time, the Republican Party became beholden to a specific religious teaching, by adopting the extreme position on abortion claimed by Evangelicals and Catholic Church leaders. The declaration that a human person exists from the moment of conception is not without controversy. Our task here is to report the findings and whatever consequences may be evident from them.

We begin our analysis of abortion roll call votes with the congressional session of 1977–1978 and conclude with the 111th Congress (2009–2010). Our examination of roll call votes reveals a pattern that emerged post-1980, with consolidation by 1990, and little or no change since then, except as a reflection of whether Democrats or Republicans were in control of the House or Senate.

The number of roll call votes on abortion in the House during the period under study has ranged from a low of six (108th Congress, 2003–2004) to a high of thirty-five (105th Congress, 1997–1998). In the Senate, the range was from two (107th Congress, 2001–2002) to twenty-three (104th Congress, 1995–1996). As was usual, House and Senate did not always vote on the same bills, and roll call votes might or might not end up as law. The Senate also voted on people for positions on courts, or cabinet positions, which might be tied to abortion questions and votes.

The sweeping Republican victory in 1994, led by Newt Gingrich, brought with it the largest number of abortion-related roll call votes in a single session, the 104th: thirty in the House and twenty-three in the Senate. On average, there were fifteen abortion-related votes in each session of the House and twelve in the Senate over this time period.[5]

In the House, pro-choice votes varied within a range of fifteen percentage points over the course of the twelve sessions, from a high of 54 percent in the 102nd (1991–1992) to a low of 39 percent in the 95th (1997–1998). In twelve of the fourteen sessions, pro-life supporters dominated the vote.

In the Senate, the proportion of pro-choice votes fluctuated within a range of fourteen percentage points, from a high of 61 percent in the 95th Congress to a low of 47 percent in the 108th (2003–2004). During this time, the House was more pro-life and the Senate more evenly split. However, examining roll call votes without taking party and religion into account tells a very incomplete story.

THE MIX OF PARTY AND RELIGION

What happens to the pattern of abortion voting when we take into account the political party affiliations of House and Senate members? Figures 4.1 and 4.2 display these patterns for the House and Senate, respectively. In the House (figure 4.1), Democrats became increasingly pro-choice, from a low average of 57 percent pro-choice votes in the 95th Congress (1977–1978) to a high of 88 percent in the 110th (2007–2008). House Republicans since 1977–1978 have been overwhelmingly pro-life, at no time exceeding 22 percent in pro-choice voting. Since the Gingrich revolution of 1994, that figure has hovered around 10 percent or lower. Thus, in the House, Democrats became more

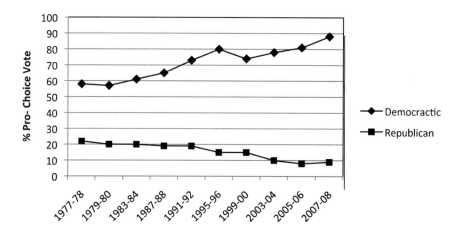

Figure 4.1. U.S. House Votes on Abortion, 1977–2008, by Party Affiliation

pro-choice over time while Republicans remained overwhelmingly pro-life. The degree of polarity—that is, the percentage differential between the party votes—more than doubled from less than 40 percent to 80 percent.

Figure 4.2 shows that in the Senate, both parties experienced change: Democrats became overwhelmingly pro-choice, from 71 percent in the 95th Congress (1977–1978) to 87 percent in the 110th (2007–2008). Republicans, meanwhile, moved from being slightly pro-choice in the 95th Congress (52 percent) to overwhelmingly pro-life, so that in the most recent sessions average support for a pro-choice position has hovered below 10 percent. Thus, in the Senate as in the House, polarization shifted away from being a clear-cut division *within* each of the two parties to a growing consensus within each party and clear polarization *between* the parties. The degree of polarity increased from less than 20 percent to more than 80 percent.

Over time—as figures 4.1 and 4.2 show—the two parties have become polarized, with the Democrats increasing their pro-choice votes. Republican votes have become even more strongly pro-life. Given the polarized and politicized position on abortion taken by the two parties, what information might the religious identity of members of the House and Senate provide that could help explain these votes? Figures 4.3 and 4.4 compare Catholic, Mainline Protestant, and Conservative Protestant votes in the House and Senate.

The religious affiliation of members of Congress does not by itself provide information about the degree to which that affiliation is or was a salient factor in their thinking or basic value orientations—in other words, we measure religious affiliation only, not religiosity. However, in an earlier study, Benson and Williams (1982) found religion in Congress to be very

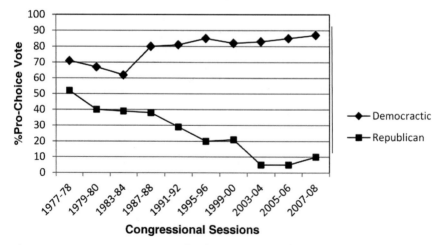

Figure 4.2.   U.S. Senate Votes on Abortion, 1977–2008, by Party Affiliation

much alive and influential in voting behavior. According to Benson and Williams, a majority of members acknowledged that their votes were influenced by their religious beliefs and values. So, at least for the 95th and 96th Congresses (1977–1980) studied by Benson and Williams and included in our own research, religion was salient to a majority of the members. Most members were reelected to the 98th Congress (1983–1984), and some still remained into the 108th Congress (2003–2004). Beyond that, we have the testimony from several members of Congress throughout their tenure in office, and especially from the 2009–2010 battle over health care reform, that speaks to the relationship between their religious beliefs and abortion. For example, we have the contrasting statements on abortion from two Roman Catholics, John Boehner (then the minority leader of the House) and Nancy Pelosi (then the majority leader of the House). Boehner stated his position in January 2006, when he was running for the position of House majority leader:

> I write you today simply for the purpose of reaffirming, proudly, that I share the commitment [to protecting the lives of the unborn and ensuring that our nation's laws reflect a belief in the sanctity of life] completely, totally and without equivocation. It is a commitment I have felt deeply throughout my life and a commitment I will uphold unapologetically if and when I am chosen to be your next Majority Leader. As a lifelong Roman Catholic and brother to eleven siblings, I believe and have always believed that life begins at conception. This is not a political position I have adopted for the sake of expedience or convenience; it is part of who I am and have always been, since long before the thought of running for office had ever entered my mind. (Quoted in Chapman 2006)

Nancy Pelosi, House majority leader, also stated her position in these words:

> As an ardent, practicing Catholic, this is an issue that I have studied for a long time. And what I know is, over the centuries, the doctors of the Church [theologians] have not been able to make that definition [when human life begins]. St. Augustine said at three months. We don't know. The point is that it shouldn't have an impact on the woman's right to choose. This isn't about abortion on demand, it's about a careful, careful consideration of all factors that a woman has to make with her doctor and her god. It is also true that God has given us, each of us, a free will and a responsibility to answer for our actions. And we want abortions to be safe, rare, and reduce the number of abortions. (Pelosi 2008)

The positions of the then House majority and minority leaders in fact mirrored closely their party's position, with the Republican House members (including all religions) almost 100 percent in line with their leader. The Democrats were not as tightly knit, as we shall see.

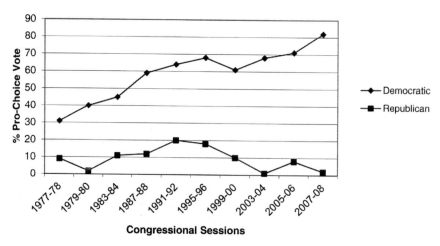

Figure 4.3a.   U.S. House Votes on Abortion, by Party and Religious Affiliation: Catholics

Figures 4.3 and 4.4 present the trends in abortion votes by religion and party for the House and Senate.[6]

THE HOUSE

Trends in abortion voting for Catholics are presented in figure 4.3a, for Mainline Protestants in 4.3b, and for Conservative Protestants in 4.3c.[7] In

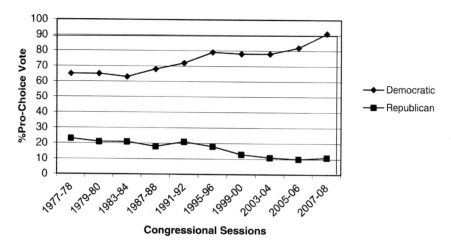

Figure 4.3b.   U.S. House Votes on Abortion, 1977–2008, by Party and Religious Affiliation, Mainline Protestants

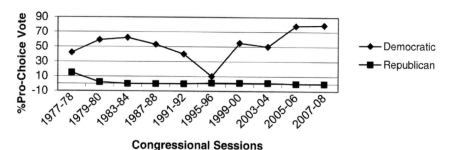

Congressional Sessions

Figure 4.3c.   U.S. House Votes on Abortion, 1977–2008, by Party and Religious Affiliation: Conservative Protestants

the House, Catholics were predominantly pro-life until the 100th Congress (1987–1988). Since then, they became increasingly pro-choice, reaching a high point in the 110th Congress (2007–2008). Mainline Protestant Democrats became increasingly pro-choice from the 95th (1977–1978) to the 110th Congress. The average annual abortion pro-choice votes among Catholics rose from 30 percent to 81 percent; among Mainline Protestants, the rise was from 65 percent to 90 percent.

The votes of Conservative Protestant Democrats have been the most volatile. A minority (41 percent) voted pro-choice in the late 1970s and early 1980s; then there were several sessions in which a majority was pro-choice. However, by the 104th session (1995–1996), those remaining in the Democratic Party were overwhelmingly pro-life. In the most recent sessions, with the election of Protestant Democrats, the move has been back to pro-choice positions. These pro-choice votes reflect the increasing presence of African American Conservative Protestant Democratic members being elected to Congress. Although these African American Democrats were members of theologically Conservative Protestant churches (on abortion), they have voting records like Catholic Democrats who are pro-choice.

Among House Republicans, Catholics were from the beginning and have remained overwhelmingly pro-life: their pro-choice votes decreased from 9 percent in the 95th Congress (1977–1978) to 2 percent in the 110th (2007–2008). Four out of five Mainline Protestant Republicans voted pro-life throughout, with the most recent pro-choice votes down near the 10 percent level; Conservative Protestants were the most consistently pro-life throughout the period, being close to 100 percent pro-life in most sessions.

Across-party polarization by religion increased for Catholics and Mainline Protestants. Conservative Protestants, both Democrats and Republicans, were moderately polarized, until the 104th Congress (1995–1996), when their votes became pro-life. By the 110th session, Conservative Protestant

Democrats had moved closer to the party position, with the degree of polarity increasing from less than 10 percent to almost 70 percent.

Figures 4.3a, b, and c make clear that the increasing polarization in the House was not the result of changes across all major religious groups. Catholic and Protestant Republicans were overwhelmingly pro-life throughout. The largest change occurred among Catholic Democrats, who became less polarized internally as pro-choice voting grew from 32 to 83 percent. Polarization also decreased among Mainline Protestant Democrats as their pro-choice votes increased by twenty-five percentage points, from 65 to 90 percent. Conservative Protestants were never internally polarized as they moved toward a consensus pro-life position in the 110th session (2007–2008).

We did not include a set of votes by Jews in the House and Senate; they have been almost consistently 100 percent pro-choice. The only House exception has been Eric Cantor (R-VA). Jewish Democrats in the House slowly increased their numbers, with all thirty-three voting pro-choice in 2010. In the Senate, ten Jewish Democrats plus two independents voted pro-choice in 2010.

A comparison of figure 4.1 with figures 4.3a, b, and c shows that the Mainline Protestant vote, by both Democrats and Republicans, most closely mirrors the party vote. The Conservative Protestant votes line up well for the Republicans, while the Democrats differ more from the party pattern until the two most recent sessions. For Catholic Democrats between the 95th (1977–1978) and the 110th Congresses, there is a polarity declining from a high near 25 percent to about 10 percent in the 110th Congress. Pro-life Catholics have been numerous enough to determine the outcomes of the great majority of House votes relating to abortion. The white Conservative Protestant Democrats have also added to the pro-life vote, as have a small percentage of Mainline Protestants.

THE SENATE, BY RELIGION AND PARTY

Figure 4.4 (a, b, c) shows that the pattern in the Senate was somewhat similar to that of the House. Senate Catholic Democrats were more pro-life than pro-choice in the immediate years after the *Roe* decision but became increasingly pro-choice, while Catholic Republicans remained overwhelmingly pro-life—leading to near total polarization with their Democratic co-religionists. A comparison of figure 4.2 with the three figures controlling for religion show again that the Mainline Protestants most closely conform to the party pattern. For the first three sessions in figures 4.2 and 4.4a, there is a declining polarity, from about 25 percent to 10 percent, of Catholic Democrats. After that, the Catholic Democrats fit well in the party vote. Catholic Republicans were

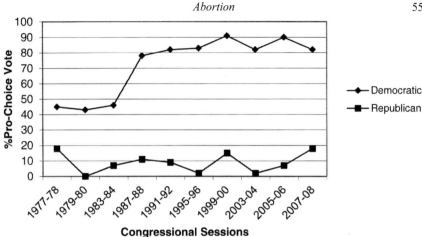

Congressional Sessions

Figure 4.4a.   U.S. Senate Votes on Abortion, 1977–2008, by Party and Religious Affiliation: Catholics

more consistently pro-life than the party itself from the late 1970s until the 106th Congress (1999–2000). In the Senate as in the House, the Conservative Protestant Republicans have been much more consistently pro-life than the party itself. The Conservative Protestant Democrats have been the most volatile.

From the 95th (1977–1978) through the 102nd Congress (1991–1992), Mainline Protestants, both Democrats and Republicans, combined with Catholic Democrats and Jews to ensure majority pro-choice votes. As Mainline

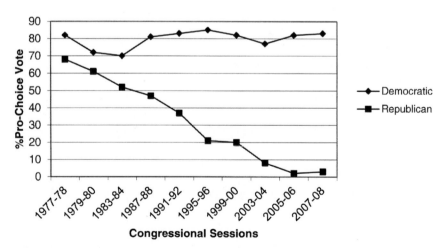

Congressional Sessions

Figure 4.4b.   U.S. Senate Votes on Abortion, 1977–2008, by Party and Religious Affiliation: Mainline Protestants

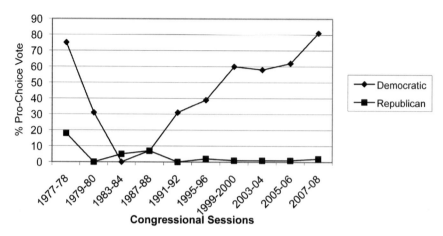

Figure 4.4c.   U.S. Senate Votes on Abortion, 1977–2008, by Party and Religious Affiliation: Conservative Protestants

Protestants became more pro-life in their votes, Catholic Democratic votes became more pro-choice, mirroring the party vote and increasing the polarity between themselves and their Republican co-religionists from 20 percent to as high as 70 percent.

Senate Mainline Protestant Democrats maintained their strongly pro-choice position above the 80 percent level throughout the study period. Conversely, Mainline Protestant Republicans underwent the largest changes. In the early years, they were almost as pro-choice as their Democratic co-religionists. However, by the 104th Congress (1995–1996), the Mainline Protestant Republicans were a pro-life majority, and by the 110th (2007–2008) their pro-choice support had dwindled to below 10 percent.

Conservative Protestant Senate Democrats changed dramatically from pro-choice before 1980 to almost 100 percent pro-life by the mid- to late 1980s to a current position that is strongly pro-choice. Conservative Protestant Republicans have remained overwhelmingly pro-life since the early post-*Roe* voting.

ANALYZING THE RELATIONSHIP BETWEEN PARTY AND RELIGION

We found a consistently high level of polarization in the roll call votes on abortion in both the House and Senate from 1977 through 2008. In the earlier period, the polarization was a mix of across- and within-party voting. That is, a significant minority of Republicans in the Senate voted pro-choice just as a significant number of Democrats voted pro-life.

When we controlled for political party, we found that on average a majority of congressional Democrats supported the pro-choice position. At the same time, on average, a majority of congressional Republicans voted pro-life. Over time, voting patterns within the parties converged, while they diverged more and more across parties. Thus, even as polarization within the House and Senate remained high, it became ever more closely identified with political party identification. Republicans became predominantly pro-life; Democrats became predominantly pro-choice.

The significant changes in voting behavior were found among Catholics and white Protestants. Congressional Catholic Democrats became strongly to overwhelmingly pro-choice while Catholic Republicans became as strongly pro-life. Strickler and Danigelis found in national surveys Catholics becoming slightly more pro-choice over time (2002, 20). Evans (2002a) found similar patterns of divergence and convergence within and between these major religious groups. Jones and Cox (chapter 7 in this book) present a compelling analysis of the Protestant-Catholic vote by party across the same time period.

The high level of polarization during the period of 1977–2008 is consistent with what DiMaggio, Evans, and Bryson (1996) reported for the opinions of those members of the public who identified closely with one or the other party. Evans (2002b) was even more emphatic, as were Hetherington (2001) and Layman and Carsey (2002).

Strickler and Danigelis (2002) found that the conservative movements of the 1980s and 1990s (family values, sanctity of life) were very effective in countering the more liberal movements of the 1970s (feminism and equal rights) and thus served to stabilize abortion attitudes, rather than seeing them evolve more into a pro-choice direction. Thus, the authors concluded that in framing public attitudes toward abortion since the 1980s, the pro-life movement led by Evangelicals and Catholic Church leaders has been more successful than the pro-choice movement in setting the terms of the public debate. As we shall see in the following pages, abortion became a major issue in the health care bill. We will show how the united vote within the Republican Party—plus the minority pro-life vote within the Democratic Party—produced a costly, antagonistic, and disruptive situation among Catholics within and outside the party.

DiMaggio, Evans, and Bryson, in their review of public opinion surveys, concluded that "whereas, in the 1970s, Republicans were less opposed to abortion than Democrats, the groups moved in opposite directions, crossing in the mid-1980s and diverging thereafter. At the same time, Republicans divided more sharply over abortion" (1996, 737).

Our findings, however, present a different picture of how abortion voting has played out in Congress; while it is true that Democrats and Republicans in Congress have been moving in opposite directions on the abortion issue, it is also true that a majority of Democrats (but not Catholics) have been pro-choice since 1979. Moreover, the DiMaggio et al. finding that Republicans in the general population were more pro-choice than the Democrats before 1980 may be accurate, but is not consistent with the people they elected, as shown by our findings (since 1999) of actual votes in Congress. Pro-choice support among Republicans in the House never exceeded 20 percent and decreased steadily toward the current level just above 10 percent. In the Senate, pro-choice Republicans declined from above 60 percent to less than 10 percent during this time. This provides further evidence of a gap between the public and the people they vote for to represent them in Congress.

Various scholars have analyzed the findings. Evans (2002b) used GSS and NES data through the year 2000 and stated that the evidence was inescapable that increasing polarization within the public may be a result of polarization in our political system. This finding was supported by Adams (1997), who noted that the abortion issue had transformed the two parties over a twenty-five-year period following *Roe v. Wade*. Furthermore, he found strong evidence that this gradual shift in Congress caused a similar change among the voting public. Hetherington makes the further point that "greater partisan polarization in Congress has clarified the parties' ideological positions for ordinary Americans, which in turn has increased party importance and salience on the mass level" (2001, 619). Using NES data for the same period, as did DiMaggio et al. (1996) and Evans (2002a, 2002b), Layman and Carsey (2002) suggested that the evolving polarization in Congress primarily impacted strong party identifiers rather than the voting masses as a whole.

Our findings on the changing religious composition of the House and Senate, along with their changing pro-choice and pro-life votes, raise questions about the direction of influence flow between the public and the members of Congress. For example, Mainline Protestant churches all have formal positions acknowledging the right to abortion at least under certain conditions. Thus, it is not surprising that Mainline Protestant Democrats have been pro-choice over the entire period, as have a minority of Republican Mainline Protestants. On the other side, the Catholic bishops have consistently condemned abortion under any and all conditions, but their impact on Catholics in the House and Senate has been mixed. There has also been a growing gap between the bishops and the Catholic public (D'Antonio et al. 2007, chapter 6; D'Antonio et al. 2013, chapters 4 and 7). Over time, congressional Catholic Democrats have become more pro-choice but Catholic Republicans have been strongly pro-life, mirroring their party and the bishops' positions. As we shall see in chapters 5 and 6 and appendix A, when it comes to key issues such as taxes, minimum wages, health care, defense spending, and the like, Catholic Democrats provide strong support for positions taken by the bishops, whereas Catholic Republicans do not.[8]

ABORTION AND THE HEALTH CARE BILL OF 2010

We conclude this chapter with an examination of the roles that religion, abortion, and party affiliation played in the Patient Protection and Affordable Care Act that passed Congress in March 2010 and was signed into law by President Obama.

During the first session of the 111th Congress (2009–2010), roll call votes on abortion-related issues covered a range of items, including the confirmation of Kathleen Sibelius as Secretary of Health and Human Services and David Hamilton to the Seventh Circuit Court of Appeals. In the Senate, the Democratic Party (with sixty votes) won all nine votes, in the process defeating a number of Republican efforts to restrict reproductive rights, in particular one that would have made it impossible for women to purchase insurance with abortion coverage in the proposed new health care exchange (even using their own funds). The effort failed and the motion to table (kill) was passed 54–45. This vote put the Senate and the House Democrats at odds on the abortion issue because on November 7, Representative Bart Stupak—a staunch pro-life Catholic from Michigan and strong supporter of health care for all Americans—had included an amendment in the House bill that would prohibit abortion coverage for individuals who received federal subsidies in the new health care system, making it inaccessible even for women who might want to use their own funds. The bill passed 240–194.

Even though the Republicans in the House had voted consistently against the health care bill, Stupak knew he could count on the Republicans to produce a solid vote (179 votes) in support of his amendment, since it was essentially a reaffirmation of the Hyde amendment that had been reauthorized every year to prevent federal funding of abortions. The only exception to the Hyde amendment was that government-funded health plans allowed payment for abortions to save the life of the mother or in instances of rape and incest.

Figures 4.3a–c show that in 2007–2008, between 10 and 25 percent of Catholic, Mainline Protestant, and Conservative Protestant Democrats regularly cast pro-life votes. Moreover, the 2008 election added additional pro-life Democrats. Stupak knew that there were at least forty Democrats who would vote against the health care bill if they were not allowed to vote on the amendment that would effectively make the Hyde amendment part of the bill. In the actual vote, sixty-two Democrats (24 percent) voted for the Stupak amendment, fitting the pattern found in figures 4.1 and 4.3a–c. Personal belief, religion, and home district helped explain their positions.

Thirteen of the seventeen amendment votes by Protestant Democrats came from seven Southern states. Only two of these Democrats were Southern Baptists. Twelve identified with one or another of the Mainline Protestant churches (Presbyterian, Lutheran, etc.). It is notable that all of the Mainline Protestant churches had theological positions that permitted their members to support abortion rights. However, it is also possible that these Southern churches were Evangelical in character despite their Mainline affiliation. Their vote may have been influenced by the conservative districts they represented, not based on any national opposition to abortion by Mainline Protestant church leaders.

Among the twenty-five Catholic Democrats who supported the Stupak amendment, twelve came from Michigan, Ohio, and Pennsylvania; three from Texas; and four from three New England states. These forty-two Democrats generally gave their votes to the pro-choice position, except when the issue involved funding or late-term abortions. Thus, the Stupak amendment showed more clearly than ever the differences between the parties on the abortion issue. Republicans could count on nearly 100 percent anti-abortion votes in the House, even though there were several moderate Republicans who occasionally cast a pro-choice vote. As figure 4.1 showed, the Democratic Party had never been able to achieve the degree of discipline on the abortion issue that the Republican Party had. Thus, the fact that 20–25 percent of the Democrats broke ranks on the abortion issue gave the Republicans a major advantage. The voting behavior of Democrats may be partially explained by the relationship between religion and the region of the country from which they come (especially Ohio, Pennsylvania, and Michigan). Many districts in these states have high percentages of pro-life Catholics and Protestants; their representatives in Congress generally reflect this reality in their voting.

The American Catholic bishops had a long history of supporting health care for all citizens. But they had also been increasingly vehement in their opposition to abortion under any and all conditions and had made their position known by increasingly and more openly criticizing Catholic officeholders who were known to be supporters of abortion rights. We have cited the issue previously; here our purpose was to provide some light on the way religion and politics had become so intertwined on the abortion issue as to threaten Catholics with sanctions on the one hand and threaten the claims to authority by the Catholic bishops on the other.

Since the Democratic Senate had passed its version of the health care bill rejecting what was essentially the Hyde amendment while the House had passed their version with the Stupak amendment, the question was how to reconcile them. The House leadership under Nancy Pelosi decided to go after the twenty-four votes needed to reconcile the House bill with the Senate bill. To do that, the leaders of both the House and Senate had to fashion a position that would guarantee that there would be no funding of abortions under the new health care bill. They argued that there was nothing in the Senate bill about funding abortions and that the Stupak amendment was not needed. After a careful study, the Catholic Health Association came out in support of the bill, followed the next day (March 16) by the Catholic bishops' strong and consistent opposition to the bill as stated.[9] By March 21, with the House leaders closing in on the magic number of 218 votes, Stupak received from President Obama a solid, ironclad guarantee that no federal funds would be used to sponsor abortion in any health care exchanges. After much tugging and pulling, the health care bill passed, on March 21, 2010.

DISCUSSION AND CONCLUSION

The way the health care bill was fought in the House and Senate is important especially as it revealed in an extraordinary way the role of religion in American politics. Catholics constitute somewhere between 21 and 25 percent of the American population. Polls by Gallup, Pew, and Jones have consistently shown that only a small minority (less than 25 percent) fully supported the bishops in their opposition to abortion. A majority supported the right of women to an abortion in some or most situations. The bishops have defined abortion in such a way that it has become a non-negotiable political item, overriding all the presumed benefits that the new health care bill would provide and which they supported. No other religious body spoke with the same impact. But no other religious body could impact the vote of the Catholic Democrats. Remember, the Republican Party was sure of voting 100 percent for the Stupak amendment; all Catholics and Protestants were aboard, and even the one Jewish member of the Republican Party was a solid member of the anti-abortion vote. The need was the twenty-five Catholic votes, and they got them along with seventeen votes from Protestant Democrats.

On the other side, the support that the Catholic Health Association provided when they decided to endorse the health care bill cannot be understated. Catholic NETWORK—a major lobbying group founded and run by women religious—as well as thousands of women religious nationally, offered their support, which helped turn the tide; the bill was then passed. So there was no lack of influence by religious groups, in this case primarily or almost exclusively Catholic on this major piece of legislation.[10]

While the bishops lost the battle over the passage of the health care bill, their opposition to it, before and since its passage, has had a continuing negative effect on the public's perception of the bill. It seems reasonable that some of the negative image a majority of the public developed toward the bill must be attributed to Stupak's amendment and the lobbying efforts of the bishops. In a larger sense, their actions did nothing to decrease the polarized condition of Congress. Meanwhile, Republicans led by Sarah Palin warned about the "death panels" that were supposedly part of the health care bill and that would allegedly decide who would live and who would die. Other Republicans warned that the bill would lead to financial ruin and would force people to purchase insurance they did not want. For their part, the Democrats failed to make a determined effort to sell their new health care bill to the public. The Democratic Senate and House leaders, but especially the president, allowed four months to pass before finally succeeding in getting the bill passed. The Republicans used those four months to create a lasting negative picture of this bill, for which the Democrats have paid dearly.

We now turn to chapter 5 where we examine roll call votes on key issues other than abortion to ascertain to what extent the polarization found on the abortion issue was reflected in key votes passed by Congress from the period 1969 (before *Roe v. Wade*) to 2008.

5

Defense, Taxes, and Welfare

Key Votes in the House and Senate

We focus now on determining whether the polarization found in abortion roll call votes (discussed in chapter 4) is also found in other key roll call votes and, if so, to what extent. We first identified significant voting issues during the 91st to 110th Congresses—that is, from 1969 to 2008. We then analyzed each issue to determine the degree of party polarization. Last, we controlled for the role of party and religion. The primary source of our congressional database of votes was the key votes selected by Michael Barone, Grant Ujifusa, and others in the *Almanac of American Politics*.[1] Most of these votes involved perennial issues, such as the budget, military spending, tax rate changes, and minimum wage increases. We briefly addressed party ideology, though most of this chapter attempts to illustrate voting differences in Congress between four voting groups: Mainline Protestants, Catholics, Conservative Protestants, and Jews.

Chapter 3 documented the changes between 1959 and 2010 in the religious composition of the House and Senate, within and between the two parties. For the first two hundred years, the U.S. Congress was dominated by Protestant men of northwestern European heritage who worshipped at Mainline Protestant churches. In essence, one ethnic group made the key decisions. Since 1959, substantial changes in members' religious affiliations in the House and Senate have altered the makeup of both parties. What voting patterns do we find with the increased diversity in religious beliefs, practices, and opinions in the Congresses between 1969 and 2008 that was brought on by increases in three of the four groups (Catholics, Conservative Protestants, and Jews)?

In examining the issues, it is important to note that, as was true with abortion votes, key votes for the House and the Senate are not always identical for a number of reasons. The legislative process can be unpredictable, and the voting schedules of the House and Senate are often not in sync. At times, either chamber might pass a bill before the other. There can also be significant differences in the content of a House bill compared with a Senate bill. Due to legislative procedures and disagreements between the House and the Senate, some of the bills on which there are key votes never actually become law but serve only as public statements or indications of support of particular members of Congress for a specified issue. For example, in the case of the opening vote on the congressional compliance bill in the 104th congressional session, the vote occurred only as a public declaration, with no intention that the bill would ever become law.[2]

FINDINGS

Across forty years of key votes, we identified and categorized them into seventeen specific issues: (1) defense spending, (2) tax cuts or reforms, (3) welfare spending or reforms, (4) civil rights, (5) law enforcement, (6) gun control, (7) the budget, (8) trade, (9) labor, (10) abortion,[3] (11) agriculture, (12) religious values, (13) campaign finance reform, (14) immigration, (15) the environment, (16) Cuba, and (17) consumer rights.

This chapter focuses on the three issues most frequently voted on during the 1969–2008 congressional sessions: (1) defense spending, (2) taxes, and (3) welfare spending. These three issues also reflect the ways in which the Democratic and Republican parties differed—that is, the Republican Party was known to be more supportive of defense spending, more supportive of tax cuts, and more opposed to welfare spending while the Democratic Party was more supportive of welfare spending, less supportive of tax cuts, and less supportive of defense spending. Our task was to ascertain whether the patterns found with the abortion votes would be repeated with these three issues. Appendix A addresses, to a more limited extent, the remaining thirteen issues. Appendix A will also show polarity figures and other ways that illustrate changes in voting behavior during the 1969–2008 congressional sessions.

DEFENSE SPENDING BILLS

Of the seventeen issues, key votes on defense spending occurred in almost every House and Senate legislative session, reflecting the prominent role the U.S. government played in global politics. In 1969, the country was heavily committed to fighting the war in Vietnam. By 2008, the war on terrorism, particularly in Iraq and Afghanistan, had contributed to substantial increases in the federal budget. U.S. involvement in wars and national security helped further entrench the armed services and the military-industrial complex in government spending programs that deeply affected the American economy and political landscape. Defense spending votes were unique because they entailed domestic and foreign policy dynamics, unlike tax cuts and welfare spending votes, which were almost exclusively domestic in nature. For example, congressional House districts with military bases or defense contractors were much more sensitive to defense spending because it directly and indirectly impacted the employment and local prosperity of their constituents.

Figure 5.1 shows the degree of polarity between House Democrats and Republicans on defense spending. Polarity is the differences between parties in support for a particular vote. For example, the first vote (which involved developing antiballistic missiles, or ABMs) in 1969 had the support of 61 percent of Republicans and 43 percent of Democrats. For this vote, the degree of polarity was the difference between Republican and Democratic support: 18 percent. During the early years (between 1969 and 1982, the Vietnam and post-Vietnam era), there was much more cross-party support on bills than ensued between 1983 and 1993 (the Reagan and first Bush presidencies). For example, from 1969 to 1983 there was only one key vote that exceeded a polarity[4] of 45 percent, and that occurred in 1978 on House Bill 9375, which approved funding for the B-1 bomber.

Not until the Reagan administration (1982) did a vote surpass 50 percent polarity; this occurred first with H.R. 6030, which involved the production of

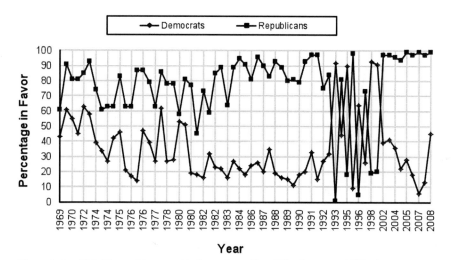

Figure 5.1. U.S. House Votes on Defense Spending Bills, by Party Affiliation

nerve gas. Between 1982 and 1989, cross-party polarization increased. After the early years of Clinton's presidency (post-1994), polarization in defense funding declined substantially and briefly began to resemble the patterns witnessed between 1969 and 1982. There were a few votes that had less than 50 percent polarity. The last such vote was in 1997, H.R. 1119 (at 46 percent), to cut funding for B-2 bombers. Since then, polarity in nearly all key votes[5] for defense spending has exceeded 50 percent. The highest polarity (92 percent) was in 2007, for H.R. 1591, to withdraw troops from Iraq.

The next set of figures shows how the three major religious groups in the House voted and compares their voting patterns with those of the parties.[6] Mainline Protestant House Republicans nearly always supported defense spending increases, as shown in figure 5.2. In fact, from 1969 to the mid-1980s they outperformed the party itself in support of defense spending increases. In the years following, they mirrored the party vote more closely. For their part, the Mainline Protestant House Democrats gave more support to increased defense spending than the Democratic Party did throughout most of these forty years. Overall, there was a greater degree of polarity in the votes of the two parties than there was between Republican and Democratic Mainline Protestants. In seven of the fifty-four key votes during these forty years, Mainline Protestant Democrats gave more support for defense spending bills than did their Republican co-religionists.

Catholic House Republicans mirrored the Republican Party fairly closely throughout these forty years, occasionally even exceeding the party's overall

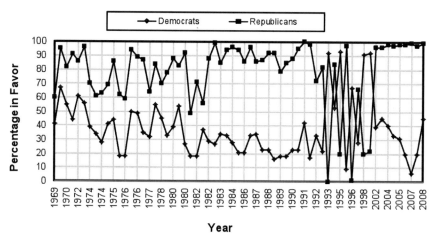

Figure 5.2.   U.S. House Votes on Defense Spending Bills, by Party and Religious Affiliation: Mainline Protestants

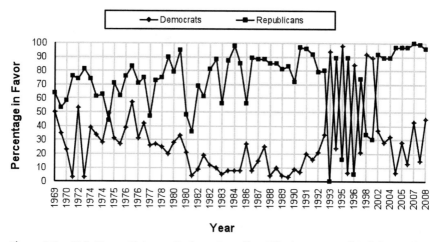

Figure 5.3. U.S. House Votes on Defense Spending Bills, by Party and Religious Affiliation: Catholics

vote, while Catholic House Democrats followed their party's voting pattern during the first ten years. During the 1980s and early 1990s, Catholic Democrats gave less support to defense spending than did the party as a whole; in the more recent votes, they resembled the rest of the Democratic Party, as overall polarization increased. Catholic Democrats were less

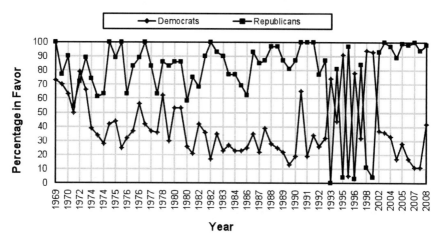

Figure 5.4. U.S. House Votes on Defense Spending Bills, by Party and Religious Affiliation: Conservative Protestants

supportive of the Cold War, particularly when foreign policy involved historically Catholic countries such as Chile, Nicaragua, El Salvador, and Cuba than in fighting the war on terrorism.

A comparison of the patterns among the Catholics showed polarities ranging between 25 percent and 65 percent in the 1970s, then gradually increasing in the 1980s and 1990s to 80 percent, and most recently to 90 percent. Among the three religious groups of Democrats, Catholics were the least likely to support increases in defense spending, while Catholic Republicans gradually became more supportive than their Mainline Protestant Republican colleagues after the 1990s.

Conservative Protestant House Republicans were the strongest supporters of legislation to increase defense spending. This was especially evident in the 1970s and early 1980s, when they exceeded the party total by 20–30 percent. They have mirrored the party more closely since the 1990s, mainly because of increased overall polarized voting. Conservative Protestant House Democrats were also more likely than other Democrats to support defense spending throughout the period 1969–2008. For example, in the 1980s Catholic Democrats consistently voted at levels below 20 percent and often at 10 percent, while Conservative Protestant Democrats frequently supported defense bills above 20 percent and often in the 30–40 percent range. Polarities between the Conservative Protestant Democrats and Republicans ranged between 40 and 60 percent in the 1970s and increased toward the 80–90 percent level thereafter. However, the medium-to-high level of support of defense spending provided an overall middle range pattern of polarity, compared with the clear polarization found in the other religious groups. Finally, there were many more Conservative Protestant Republicans as a proportion of party representatives than in the case of Conservative Protestant Democrats.

THE JEWISH VOTE

Voting trends among Jews in the House must be read with caution for two reasons: (1) until recently there was not a sufficient number of Jewish representatives to allow for meaningful comparisons, and (2) there was only one Jewish House Republican in the most recent years. Thus, extreme polarization might reflect, at times, the vote of a single Jewish Republican.

In terms of defense-related votes, Jews were united in the House in voting against arms sales to Saudi Arabia. Democratic Jews in the House were initially more supportive of the Iraq war and the war on terrorism than were other Democrats. In contrast, the few Jews in Congress in the 1960s and 1970s were generally the least likely in either party to support the Vietnam

War or post–Vietnam era spending. Also, Jews were strongly supportive of limiting nuclear testing, but were more likely to fund Strategic Defense Initiative programs than other Democrats. Thus, in certain defense-related matters pertaining to U.S. foreign policy, Democratic Jews represented a more independent voice: with the exception of votes pertaining to the Middle East or Israel, Jewish Democrats were less supportive of defense spending bills than the Democratic Party as a whole.

We will explore some of the reasons for these votes in chapter 8. The number of Jewish House Democrats during this forty-year period ranged from a low of nine in 1959 to a high of thirty in 2008. In addition, there has been a consistent increase in the number of Jewish Democrats while the number of Jewish House Republicans has declined.

VOTING IN THE SENATE

Next, in figures 5.5, 5.6, 5.7, and 5.8 we examine Senate votes on defense spending bills between 1969 and 2008.

The first pattern that emerged from the data was that Senate Republicans were more than twice as likely as Democrats to support increases in defense spending. The polarities between Republicans and Democrats ranged from lows of 10 percent or less in the 1970s to as high as 100 percent after 2005. Between 1982 and 1991 (the Reagan and first George Bush years), no more than 40 percent of Senate Democrats supported defense spending increases.

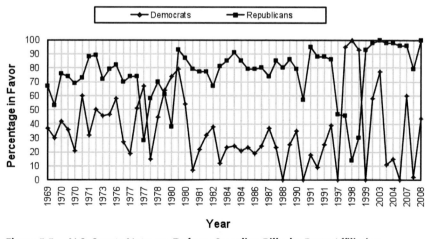

Figure 5.5.   U.S. Senate Votes on Defense Spending Bills, by Party Affiliation

During the Clinton years (1993–2000) Democratic support for defense spending varied considerably from less than 10 percent to nearly 100 percent. This inconsistent Democratic support continued between 2001 and 2005 under President George W. Bush. Republicans, on the other hand, gave almost 100 percent support to all defense bills after 2001. Democratic support generally increased during Democratic presidencies (Carter and Clinton) as a response to their party's foreign policies, while Republican support of defense spending remained strong during Democratic presidencies.

Mainline Protestant Democratic senators were more likely than other Senate Democrats to support defense spending throughout the period 1969–2008. Occasionally, such as during the 1970s, before the Reagan presidency, Mainline Protestant Democrats were more supportive of defense spending increases than were their Republican co-religionists. This voting pattern reemerged in the Clinton presidency, when Mainline Protestant Democrats were again more supportive of military funding (e.g., for the military operations in Bosnia) than were Mainline Protestant Republicans. The decline in numbers of Mainline Protestant Democrats in the Senate coincided with increased polarity between the parties. During the 1970s, the polarities among the Mainline Protestants ranged from a low of 10 percent to highs of 60 percent. Polarization increased during the Reagan years and increased again during the Clinton and George W. Bush years.

Catholic Republican senators were more likely than the Republican Party as a whole to give maximum support to increases in defense spending. However, on three votes during the 1970s, they gave no support to pending

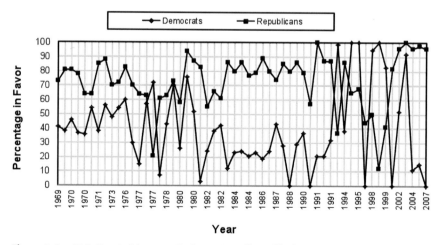

Figure 5.6. U.S. Senate Votes on Defense Spending Bills, by Party and Religious Affiliation: Mainline Protestants

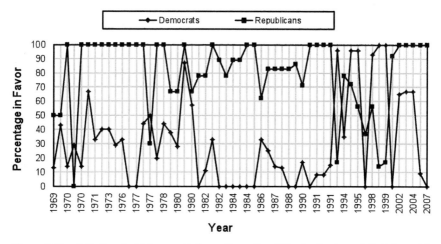

Figure 5.7. U.S. Senate Votes on Defense Spending Bills, by Party and Religious Affiliation: Catholics

legislation.[7] By the 1980s, Catholic Republican senators began to vote more with the party, and from the period after 2000, when polarization peaked, they mirrored the party overall. Like Catholic House Republicans, Catholic Senate Republicans were more likely than Senate Democrats to support defense spending. Among Catholic Republican senators, over half of the votes between 1969 and 2008 were between 90 percent and 100 percent in support of increased military spending. What was equally impressive was that the proportion of support did not decline but increased as the number of Catholic Republican senators grew between the 91st and 110th sessions. This was in sharp contrast to Catholic Democrats, who regularly voted against defense spending when compared with any other group. Nearly half of the total defense spending votes (twenty-four) by Catholic Democrats had a support level of 10 percent or less.

Overall, Catholics appeared to be the most polarized of all the religious groups during parts of the sessions of the 1970s, the 1980s, and 1990s and into the years of the George W. Bush administration.

After 1980, a higher percentage of Conservative than Mainline Protestant Republican senators began to support defense spending. Perhaps reflecting their initially insignificant numbers in the Senate, Conservative Protestants were the least likely among Republican senators to support defense spending during the Vietnam and post-Vietnam era. This contrasts with Conservative Protestant Democratic senators, who were more likely than other Democrats to support such spending.

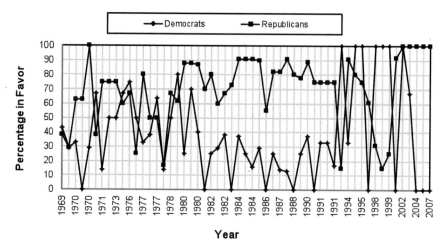

Figure 5.8. U.S. Senate Votes on Defense Spending Bills, by Party and Religious Affiliation: Conservative Protestants

As a group of co-religionists in the Senate, particularly in the 1960s and 1970s, Conservative Protestants—Democrats and Republicans alike—were the least polarized. Polarization among Conservative Protestants began in 1980 (prior to the House divide that occurred after the 1982 election) but never reached the degree of polarity experienced among Catholics.

JEWISH VOTES IN THE SENATE

Jewish senators' voting data has the same limitation as existed among Jews in the House: (1) the number of Jewish senators was until recently too small to make voting comparisons meaningful, and (2) though there were more Jewish senators in recent years, there were no Jewish Republican senators as of 2010, and there were very few in past years. Thus, the extreme polarization from one vote to another reflected, at times, a single Jewish Republican. What was unique in analyzing Jewish Democrats was that they sometimes supported defense spending more strongly than did other Democrats. Therefore, while partisan differences could not be measured, Jewish Democrats as a group tended to support defense spending more predictably than did their Democratic colleagues as a whole. We turn now to congressional votes on taxes.

TAXES

Figures 5.9 through 5.16 show the percentages of House and Senate members who supported tax bills. Tax votes showed a strong partisan divide. The typical Democratic policy position was that increasing tax rates for higher income citizens is fair because of the privileged social and economic position they enjoy. The typical Republican policy response (especially since Reagan) was that higher income taxpayers should be allowed to stimulate the economy by privately investing their incomes. Ideologically, Democrats often viewed tax cuts or reforms as a cost to the government's ability to promote the common good, while Republicans viewed such tax cuts as a path to fiscal health.

While some tax votes favored lower- and middle-class taxpayers, with few exceptions they disproportionally benefited higher-income taxpayers. In figures 5.9, 5.10, 5.11, and 5.12 we examine House votes on tax bills between 1969 and 2008.

Figure 5.9 indicates persistent party polarization on key tax votes between 1970 and 2005. The absence of polarization in the 1970s may be attributed to the lack of effort to reduce or to reform taxes. For example, there were fewer key votes in the 1970s that involved reducing taxes. Only one vote to reduce marginal tax rates, the 1986 tax reform bill—championed by Illinois Democratic representative Dan Rostenkowski—had slightly more support from Democrats than Republicans. The only other nonpolarized vote (in 1970, on increasing commuter taxes) that had less support from Democrats than Republicans was partly because it directly cost workers, and the unions

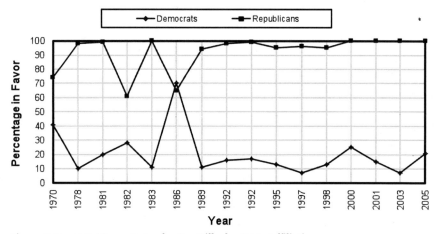

Figure 5.9. U.S. House Votes for Tax Bills, by Party Affiliation

opposed it. More prominent is the almost 100 percent approval by Republicans to reduce taxes or to oppose increasing taxes. Figure 5.9 shows that the last four votes between 2001 and 2005 (two on eliminating inheritance taxes and two on reducing income taxes) received 100 percent Republican support.

Regarding tax reform, Republicans were proactive in attempting to reduce taxes, with Democrats mainly refusing to cooperate or to initiate tax reductions or reform. However, a consistent number of Democrats (between 10 and 25 percent) agreed with Republicans on tax issues. For example, Democrats never reached zero percent in support of tax cuts or against raising taxes, while Republicans routinely either achieved consensus or came very close to it throughout the period of study. It is clear that tax reductions were a core part of Republican ideology while Democrats were more ideologically flexible about whether to support a tax bill or not.

How did religious affiliation influence congressional voting on taxes? How often did Republicans of specific denominations vote to increase taxes and how often did Democrats of specific denominations vote to decrease or to eliminate taxes on higher-income taxpayers or the wealthy?

Figure 5.10 shows that Mainline Protestant House Republicans were less supportive of tax cuts than was the party as a whole in the 1970s, with polarities ranging between 10 percent and 40 percent. Beginning in the late 1980s, the Republican Party moved toward 100 percent solidarity in support of all tax bills, with Mainline Protestant House Democrats gradually mirroring them. Mainline Protestant Democrats gave majority support to tax bills on only two occasions in the 1970s, but their support was enough to ensure

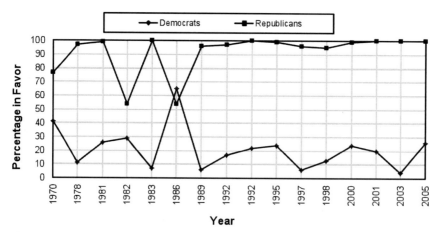

Figure 5.10.   U.S. House Votes on Tax Bills, by Party and Religious Affiliation: Mainline Protestants

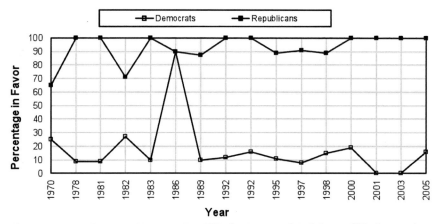

Figure 5.11.   U.S. House Votes on Tax Bills, by Party and Religious Affiliation: Catholics

passage of the legislation. Otherwise, their voting often mirrored their party's overall pattern. However, Mainline Protestant House Democrats were more likely to break with their party to support tax cuts.

Among Catholics in the House, as figure 5.11 indicates, Democrats and some Republicans were reluctant to agree on tax cuts. Ten percent of Catholic Republicans in the House voted differently from the rest of the party. This is not as striking as the abortion vote findings, but it is consistent enough in

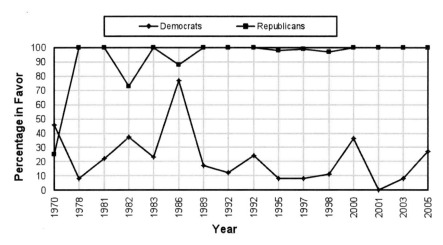

Figure 5.12.   U.S. House Votes on Tax Bills, by Party and Religious Affiliation: Conservative Protestants

comparison with Conservative and Mainline Protestants to show an independent streak and the possible influence of Catholic Church teachings as they related to social spending. The only tax cut that showed more support from Democrats than from Republicans was the 1986 Tax Reform Act pushed through by a Catholic House Democrat, Representative Dan Rostenkowski.

Figure 5.12 shows that with the same three exceptions (1970, 1982, and 1986) polarities between Conservative Democrats and Republicans ranged from 60 to 100 percent. This should be no surprise given the Republican Party support for the Norquist "no taxes" pledge. As a group, Conservative Protestant House Republicans were the most likely to support tax cuts after 1980. Prior to the election of Reagan, they were less likely to support tax cuts than Catholic or Mainline Protestant House Republicans. Among Democrats, Conservative and Mainline Protestants were most likely to support tax cuts while Catholics were least likely. Thus, among House Democrats tax cuts were supported more by Mainline and Conservative Protestants than by Catholics and Jews. Figures 5.13, 5.14, 5.15, and 5.16 display Senate votes on tax bills between 1969 and 2008.

In the Senate, between 1969 and 1986, polarities between the parties ranged between 10 and 80 percent. After 1986, polarities increased to an average of almost 75 percent. Democratic support for tax bills declined to a range between 0 percent and 25 percent. There were two votes with more Democrats than Republicans supporting tax bills. The votes were in 1971, on tax equalization for single taxpayers, and in 1982, to increase a tax to pay for roads and highways. The last Senate tax bill that received substantial Democratic support was the same one as in the House, the tax reform of 1986. Since

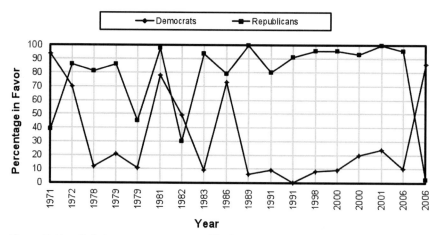

Figure 5.13.   U.S. Senate Votes on Tax Bills, by Party Affiliation

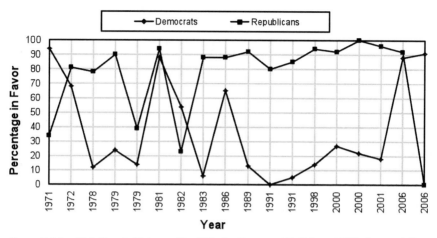

Figure 5.14. U.S. Senate Votes on Tax Bills, by Party and Religious Affiliation: Mainline Protestants

then, only the 2006 vote, which involved lowering tax liability for liquidating retirement plans (in some cases), had more than 20 percent support among Democratic senators.

From 1969 through the early 1980s, Mainline Protestant senators had polarities ranging from less than 10 percent to about 70 percent. After 1986, polarities increased to levels as high as 80 and even 90 percent. The voting

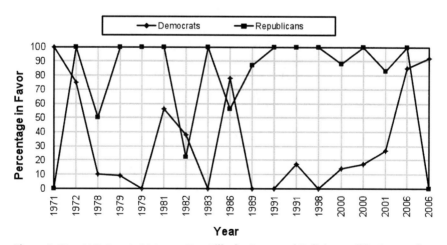

Figure 5.15. U.S. Senate Votes on Tax Bills, by Party and Religious Affiliation: Catholics

pattern of Mainline Protestant Republicans more closely mirrored the party votes than did those of Mainline Protestant Democrats, who often deviated from the party by more than 5 or 10 percent in support of tax cuts or reform.

Overall, Catholic Republican senators were more likely than the Republican Party as a whole to give 100 percent support for tax bills. However, there were two bills to reduce taxes during this period that received zero percent support from Catholic Republican senators. The first one, in 1971, was the vote to treat single and married taxpayers alike. The second one, in 2006, was a bill to reduce taxes on withdrawals from retirement accounts. Yet, on most occasions through the 1970s to the 1990s, Catholic Republicans led their party on tax votes.

Catholic Republican senators mirrored the party once polarization increased to its peak levels after 2000. The proportion of support for tax cuts in fact increased as the number of Catholic Republican senators grew between 1969 and 2006. This was in sharp contrast with Catholic Democratic senators who voted against tax cuts more than any other group. Overall, Catholics in the Senate were the most polarized of all the religious groups throughout most of the congressional sessions examined in this study.

The level of polarity between Conservative Protestant Republican senators[8] and their Democratic co-religionists was lower than that of the parties in general during the Vietnam and post-Vietnam era (between 1969 and 1979). However, after 1980 Conservative Protestant Republicans began to support tax cut bills as much as or more than Republican senators in general. Support of tax cuts among Conservative Protestant Republican senators increased

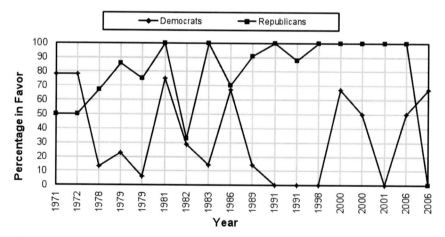

Figure 5.16.   U.S. Senate Votes on Tax Bills, by Party and Religious Affiliation: Conservative Protestants

as their overall numbers in the Senate increased throughout the 1980s, while support of tax cuts among Mainline Protestant Republican senators decreased. The high level of polarity between the Conservative Republicans and Democrats after 1989 was interrupted on four occasions: in each case, Conservative Democrats supported these four bills by votes ranging between 50 and 70 percent.

Jewish senators generally supported the Democratic Party's position opposing tax cuts.

We turn now to voting on welfare bills.

WELFARE

Welfare votes focused specifically on government spending for programs such as food stamps, Social Security, Medicare, and a variety of other welfare reform bills. Figure 5.17 presents the votes by party. Figures 5.18 through 5.20 show how each religious group, by party, voted on welfare spending bills in the House.

The finding of note in figure 5.17 is the reversal in the party voting patterns. The Democrats were the party supporting welfare bills. Between 1969 and 1978, polarities ranged from 5 percent to 70 percent. Beginning in 1987, almost all votes yielded polarities above the 70 percent level.

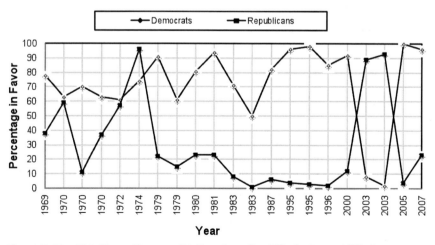

Figure 5.17.   U.S. House Votes on Welfare Spending Bills, by Party Affiliation

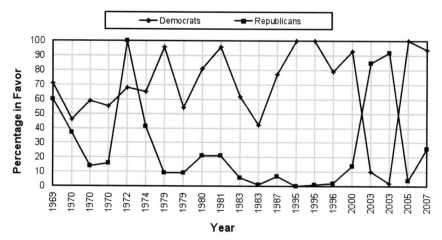

Figure 5.18. U.S. House Votes on Welfare Spending Bills, by Party and Religious Affiliation: Mainline Protestants

From 1969 to 1979, Mainline Protestant House Republicans and Democrats were generally less supportive of welfare spending bills than were their parties overall. This distinction began to fade into the 1980s as polarity increased. By the end of the 1980s, it became very difficult to determine any noticeable difference between Mainline Protestant voting in the House and

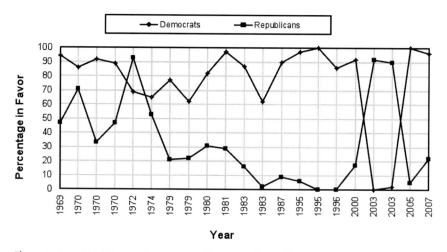

Figure 5.19. U.S. House Votes on Welfare Spending Bills, by Party and Religious Affiliation: Catholics

their overall party voting. This similarity continued throughout the 1990s and 2000s, despite the fact that the overall number of Mainline Protestants in the House declined substantially since the 1980s. As a group, Mainline Protestant Republicans were the least supportive of welfare spending. On the other hand, Mainline Protestant Democrats generally mirrored their party vote, so that the polarity with their Republican co-religionists often reached 100 percent.

Catholic members of the House, both Republicans and Democrats, were consistently more supportive of welfare spending bills throughout the period of study than were Mainline Protestants. Though overall polarization increased, Catholic House Republicans were more likely to break from the Republican Party to support welfare such as health insurance for children, and very rarely did Catholic House Democrats break away from the Democratic Party to vote against welfare spending.[9] The distinction was more pronounced in 1969–1979, when there was less polarization between parties. Religion's influence on House voting may have declined in favor of party partisanship since 1980 (especially in the 1980s), but it still played a role in the area of welfare spending.

Conservative Protestant members of the House were the counterweight to Catholics. In the 1969–1979 period and extending into the mid-1980s, Conservative Protestants (Democrats and Republicans) were the least likely to support welfare spending bills. When polarization increased in the 1990s and 2000s, Conservative Protestant House Democrats gave less support than any other group of Democrats for welfare spending, while Republicans were

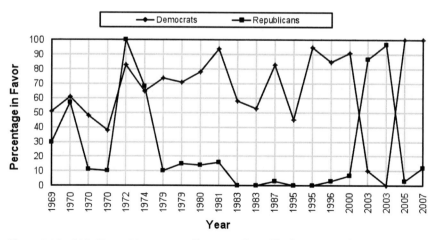

Figure 5.20 U.S. House Votes on Welfare Spending Bills, by Party and Religious Affiliation: Conservative Protestants

even more likely to vote against welfare spending. Thus, the level of polarity across parties remained high. In matters of ideology regarding welfare, it would seem that the Mainline Protestants represented the moderates of either party. The trend of more Conservative Protestants, Catholics, and Jews becoming elected to the House in proportion to the overall number probably helped to reinforce the increasing polarization within Congress and within American society in general with two very different views on welfare and the role of government in society.

As expected, Jewish House Democrats either mirrored or led the Democratic Party in support of welfare legislation.

Next, in figures 5.21, 5.22, 5.23, and 5.24 we examine Senate votes on welfare spending bills between 1969 and 2008.

Between 1974 and 1980 (figure 5.21), polarities between parties in Senate voting ranged from 50 percent to 30 percent. After 1980, there were only two votes with polarities under 50 percent. Much of this decreased polarization in the pre-Reagan years can be explained by the fact that there were few efforts to curb entitlement and social program spending. However, since the early 1980s, one party, the Republican Party, continually attempted to curb welfare spending, while the other party, the Democratic Party, continually either refused to vote for cuts or supplied bills to expand welfare spending. The parties clearly moved in different directions, starting with the Reagan revolution of the 1980s and the Republican-led Congresses of the 1990s into the 2000s.

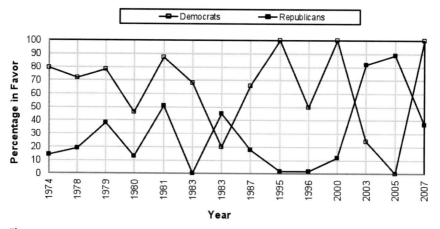

Figure 5.21.   U.S. Senate Votes on Welfare Spending Bills, by Party Affiliation

Mainline Protestant Senate Welfare Votes

Welfare spending votes of Mainline Protestant senators were mixed. Some Republican measures, such as a 1995 measure to slow the growth of Medicare, received bipartisan support. A 90 percent polarization between Mainline Protestant Democratic and Republican senators happened only twice, in 1985 and 2005. Unlike in the House, Mainline Protestant members of the Senate frequently supported the other party's initiatives. Republican-led welfare cuts between 1980 and 1999 showed that some Mainline Protestant Republicans often voted for welfare increases despite the party's opposition to welfare spending. Conversely, for only the last two votes under Harry Reid's leadership was there nearly 100 percent support for welfare increases among Mainline Protestant Democrats. Prior to that, only once did Democrats receive a 90 percent or greater level of support from Mainline Protestant Democrats. Thus, Mainline Protestant Democrats were the least likely to support welfare spending, which followed the same pattern as Mainline Protestant House Democrats.

Senate Catholic Support for Welfare Bills

In the 1970s, there were some votes that demonstrated practical measures taken by Catholic Democrats. For example, in the 95th session (1975–1976)

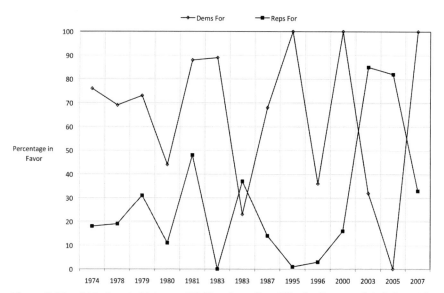

Figure 5.22   U.S. Senate Votes on Welfare Spending Bills, by Party and Religious Affiliation: Mainline Protestants

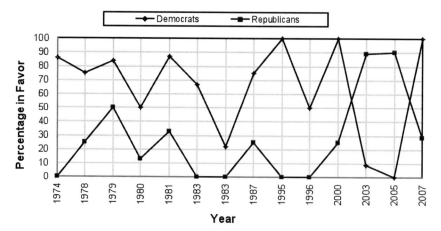

Figure 5.23.   U.S. Senate Votes on Welfare Spending Bills, by Party and Religious Affiliation: Catholics

75 percent of Catholic Democratic senators (in contrast to 50 percent of Republicans) supported hospital cost containment measures. Catholic Democrats were also as unwilling as Republicans to support minimum wage for domestic workers. Catholic Republicans, just as Catholics in the House in certain circumstances, also cast their votes against the party line, thus conforming to some Catholic teachings on social justice. For example, nearly 70 percent of Catholic Republican senators voted against cutting funding for housing for the elderly in 1985.

In 1987, again 70 percent of Catholic Republican senators supported increasing the minimum wage. In both of these cases, among Mainline Protestant Republicans there was less than 15 percent support. Later, in 2003, 90 percent of Catholic Republicans voted against curbing entitlement spending; yet 100 percent of Mainline Protestant Republican senators voted for cutting entitlement spending. Catholic Republican senators supported such curbs.

Beginning in 1983, polarity in the Senate often exceeded 90 percent. But there were exceptions, such as a bill to forgive third-world debt and for insurance for children, both of which received support from some Catholic Republicans. This willingness to break with their party may reflect their support for the Church's social teachings.

Since 1995 Catholic Democratic senators have consistently displayed 100 percent support for efforts to increase welfare spending or to prevent its decrease.[10] This has stood out especially in comparison to Mainline Protestant

Democrats, whose support only recently began to exceed over 90 percent. Catholic Democrats did not always initiate increases in welfare spending. For example, in 2003 the Medicare prescription option was initiated by President George W. Bush. Only 10 percent of Catholic Democratic senators voted with the Republican Party, even though it represented an increase in entitlement spending, which they usually supported. A major objection was that the prescription drug bill was unfunded.

In 1995, there was a united vote to curb rising Medicare costs on which all Catholics, Democratic and Republican, agreed. This was a practical vote based on the general acknowledgment that Medicare costs were rising at an alarming rate. A vote to control these costs could enable more funding to be allocated to other social programs. Therefore, a containment-of-cost vote may not have been seen as a vote against welfare spending but as a vote for the continued survival of the Medicare program and the funding of other programs.

On votes to increase welfare spending, Conservative Protestant senators contributed more to party polarization than Catholics did (as expected). Since 1981, with the exception of the George W. Bush–sponsored Medicare prescription option, Conservative Protestant Republican senators rarely gave more than 10 percent of their votes to increase welfare spending. In comparison with Catholic Republican senators, whose support ranged between 20 and 35 percent, Conservative Protestant Republican senators gave no support.

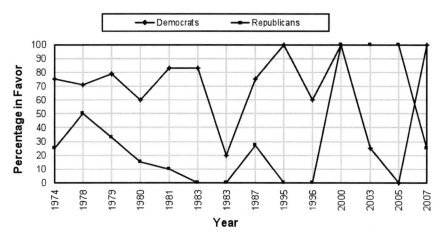

Figure 5.24.   U.S. Senate Votes on Welfare Spending Bills, by Party and Religious Affiliation: Conservative Protestants

The difference was apparent, especially when the Republicans' control of Congress in 1995 was taken into account.

Efforts to reduce welfare spending by Conservative Protestant Republicans were matched by efforts to sustain or to increase welfare spending by Catholic Democrats. As noted with Catholic Republican senators who voted 100 percent with Catholic Democrats to support Medicare growth, only 10 percent of Conservative Protestant Republican senators voted with their Democratic counterparts. The division on welfare spending between Conservative Protestants was very clear. Conservative Protestant senators, unlike Conservative Protestants in the House, as a group were much more partisan and more polarized on welfare spending. The independent nature of most Conservative Protestant churches (which tend to be congregational rather than have a hierarchical management structure) may explain these disparities, but the length of Senate terms (six years) may also be a factor. Again, the intriguing result was that Conservative Protestant membership in the Senate contributed disproportionately to partisan behavior, which may or may not be due to religious factors.

JEWS IN CONGRESS

As noted in chapters 2 and 3, Jews historically had an insignificant presence in Congress, but in recent decades their numbers, particularly in the Democratic Party, significantly increased. While Jewish Democrats have always outnumbered Jewish Republicans, in the 1960s and 1970s there was a greater balance of Jews across the parties. Due to the limited number of Republican Jews in Congress between 1971 and 2008, their voting must be seen as having minimal impact. However, among Democrats, Jewish senators have consistently supported welfare legislation with their party.

SUMMARY AND CONCLUSION

In this chapter, we examined whether—and to what extent—political parties and religious affiliation became polarized on three key issues that reflected the ideological differences in the two parties' visions of the good society. We tracked the voting patterns of both parties, citing the growing levels of polarization over time on defense spending, taxes, and welfare spending. Next, we examined the party members by their religious affiliation to look for evidence of a religious factor in voting. Our findings indicated that Mainline Protestants were the least partisan of the four religious groups in our study.

Mainline Protestant Republicans were more likely to vote independently from other Republicans, and Mainline Protestant Democrats were more likely to vote independently from other Democrats than members of other religious affiliations. The decrease in the number of Mainline Protestants from parts of the country other than the South may help explain some of the increased polarization that has characterized Congress in recent decades.

6

Does Religion Transcend Social Issue Voting?

The Relationship between Religion and Congressional Ideology

Steven A. Tuch and Alyx Mark

"When people in positions of power and influence don't bring their Christian beliefs into the equation, what's the point of saying you're a Christian?"

"I . . . believe that [political leaders] should keep their religious beliefs separate from making policy decisions and uphold the Constitution."

These quotes, reported in a *Washington Post* article (August 25, 2012) about the role of faith in politics, are from a small, nonrandom sample of respondents in the state of Virginia who were asked the question, "Do you think a political leader should rely on his or her religious beliefs in making policy decisions?" The views of these two interviewees represent polar opposites on a continuum of the preferred connection between religion and policymaking. What can we discern about which view more closely reflects the actual process by which legislators deliberate over, and ultimately cast, their votes? That is the question we address in this chapter by examining the totality of congressional roll call votes between 1969 and 2010.

As discussed in previous chapters, much of the culture wars literature has focused on the issue of abortion. In chapter 5, we analyzed Barone and Ujifusa's key votes to determine whether abortion is a uniquely polarizing issue or, rather, an exemplar of a larger trend. In this chapter we broaden the focus even further. The goals of the chapter are twofold: first, to determine if the polarization that characterizes voting on abortion and on key issues persists when all congressional roll call votes—as opposed to a select few—are examined; and second, if polarization does persist, to determine whether religion plays a discernible role in shaping it. We analyze data for the 91st through the 111th congressional sessions (1969–2010).

THE CHANGING RELIGIOUS
COMPOSITION OF THE HOUSE AND SENATE

Chapter 3 presented a detailed analysis of changes in the religious affiliations of House and Senate members over the past half century. As noted, between 1960 and 2010 the number of Liberal and Moderate Protestants in the House decreased substantially, Catholics increased their numbers by about a third, Jews tripled their representation, and Conservative Protestants grew to nearly a fifth of the House.[1] In the Senate, the number of Mainline Protestants declined substantially over this period, Catholics more than doubled their representation, Jews increased more than sixfold, and Conservative Protestants increased their representation to nearly a quarter of the Senate.

Table 6.1 summarizes changes between 1969 and 2010 in the representation of Conservative Protestants in the House and Senate, separately by party.[2]

Among Democrats, the percentage of Conservative Protestants in the House fluctuated only slightly over this forty-year period but increased substantially—from 17.8 percent to 30.1 percent—among Republicans. In the Senate, analogously, Conservative Protestants saw their representation decline by more than half among Democrats—from 19.9 percent to 9.1 percent—while registering a 5.5 percent gain among Republicans. Thus, over-time change in the proportion of members who are affiliated with Conservative Protestant religious denominations has occurred in both chambers, though in opposite directions—declining among Democrats (especially in the Senate) and increasing among Republicans (in both the House and Senate).

Table 6.1.   Conservative Protestants by Chamber and Party, 1970–2010

House	Democrats	Republicans
1970s*	19.0	17.8
1980s	16.7	20.0
1990s	20.0	27.3
2000s	18.6	30.1

Senate	Democrats	Republicans
1970s	19.9	20.8
1980s	16.5	22.7
1990s	10.1	22.4
2000s	9.1	26.3

* Includes the 91st Congress

What has been the impact on polarization of this forty-year pattern of conservative Protestants leaving the ranks of the Democratic Party while simultaneously increasing their numbers in the Republican Party? In order to address this question we utilize Poole's (1998) Common Space NOMINATE scores as a measure of legislator ideology. Common Space scores provide an across-chamber measure of ideology by independently scaling each member's roll call votes in a given congressional session using members who have served in both chambers as "bridge" observations. In the Common Space methodology, there are 636 members of Congress who have served in both the House and the Senate. These members serve to link the two chambers for comparison, forming a "bridge" between them. This scaling represents a member's average ideal point based upon his or her vote choices in that session, the logic being that an individual legislator will vote "yea" or "nay" on a particular bill based on its location relative to the member's ideal point. Thus, an aggregation of these choices will represent a close approximation of a member's ideology. Member ideology is represented in two-dimensional space—the first dimension capturing the contemporary liberal-conservative split in Congress and the second capturing a host of social issues voting. While a two-dimensional measure is of importance during certain eras, in modern times most voting can be explained by the first dimension, with positive scores indicating more conservative members and negative scores indicating more liberal members. As a result, for this analysis we utilize the first dimension, which closely approximates D-NOMINATE values for members of Congress. D-NOMINATE scores use roll call votes of members of Congress as a tool to develop estimations of a member's ideal point on issues related to the economy, which is best known as the "first dimension" of NOMINATE values. As previously noted, this dimension explains much of the voting behavior of the modern Congress. There are several different NOMINATE scaling measures used currently by congressional scholars, but for our purposes it is important to utilize the Common Space measure in order to make comparisons across chambers and time.

Table 6.2 shows that Democrats in both the House and Senate displayed monotonic increases in liberal voting from 1970 to 2010, with average ideology scores ranging from −.3025 to −.4048 in the House and from −.3063 to −.3289 in the Senate. The trend among Republicans was in the opposite direction, one of steady increases in conservative voting, from .2717 to .4321 in the House and from .2619 to .3814 in the Senate. These scores also indicate that the pace of ideological change differed by party. House Republicans became more conservative at a faster pace ($.4321 - .2717 = .1604$) than their Democratic counterparts became more liberal ($|.4808 - .3025| = .1023$). The comparable figures for Senate Republicans ($.3814 - .2619 = .1195$) and Democrats ($|.3289 - .3063| = .0226$) reveal the same pattern.

Chapter 6

Table 6.2.   Average Ideology Scores by Chamber and Party, 1970–2010

House	Democrats	Republicans
1970s*	−.3025	.2717
1980s	−.3189	.3303
1990s	−.3675	.3832
2000s	−.4048	.4321

Senate	Democrats	Republicans
1970s*	−.3063	.2619
1980s	−.3074	.3248
1990s	−.3238	.3506
2000s	−.3289	.3814

* Includes the 91st Congress

Although we cannot unequivocally attribute the increase in liberal voting among Democrats to the departure of Conservative Protestants from their ranks, nor the increase in conservative voting among Republicans to the influx of Conservative Protestants into their ranks, the correlations between ideology and religion displayed in table 6.3 suggest that such an attribution is plausible.

The correlation between religion and (liberal) ideology was strongest for Catholic legislators in the 1970s and for Jewish legislators in every decade since, as well as over the entire timeline. Analogously, the correlation between religion and (conservative) ideology was strongest for Conservative Protestants in the two most recent decades, as well as overall. Moreover, between the 1970s and 2000s, the magnitudes of the correlations increased monotonically among Jews and, since the 1980s, among Catholics; among Moderate Protestants the correlations monotonically decreased; and among Conservative Protestants and, since the 1980s, Liberal Protestants, they monotonically increased.

Table 6.3.   Correlations between Ideology and Religion, by Decade

	1970s	1980s	1990s	2000s	Total
Catholic[†]	−0.243*	−0.151*	−0.156*	−0.180*	−0.172*
Jewish	−0.153*	−0.166*	−0.233*	−0.253*	−0.205*
Liberal Protestant	0.142*	0.090*	0.119*	0.144*	0.111*
Moderate Protestant	0.106*	0.094*	0.068*	0.061*	0.077*
Conservative Protestant	0.057*	0.078*	0.125*	0.165*	0.117*

† Coded 1 for Catholics, 0 otherwise; and analogously for the other religious groups

* $p < .05$

Table 6.4. Average Polarization Scores by
Chamber, 1970–2010

	House	Senate
1970s*	.5742	.5682
1980s	.6492	.6322
1990s	.7507	.6744
2000s	.8369	.7103

* Includes the 91st Congress

What is the extent of polarization between Democrats and Republicans when all roll call votes are analyzed? What has been the trend since the 1970s? Table 6.4 displays trends in ideological polarization by chamber. Polarization scores were calculated by subtracting the average Common Space score among Democrats from the average score among Republicans in each decade.[3] The differences show steady increases in polarization within and across chambers since 1969. In the House, polarization ranged from a low of .5742 in the 1970s to a high of .8369 in the 2000s, a range of .2627; the corresponding figures in the Senate were .5682 and .7103, a range of .1421. As Poole notes, polarization in both chambers has not been higher since Reconstruction ended.

MULTIVARIATE ANALYSES

We turn our attention next to a series of multivariate models. Tables 6.5 and 6.6 display the results of regressing Common Space scores on several explanatory variables in the House and Senate, respectively. Model 1 in each table shows unstandardized regression coefficients for a baseline model that includes only party, model 2 removes party and fits a series of dummy variables for religion (Catholics are the reference group), model 3 fits both party and religion, and model 4 (the "full" model) increments the party and religion model with controls for several member and district (in table 6.5) or state (in table 6.6) characteristics that might help explain any religion-ideology association. Gender (1 = female), though not usually found by previous research to impact ideology, is nevertheless included in order to capture any potential gender differences over time (see Welch [1985] and Vega and Firestone [1995]). Democratic vote share in the last presidential election serves as a proxy for constituent ideology in a representative's district or senator's state. The rationale for including a measure of constituent ideology is that a member's ideology might be influenced by the degree to which her or his district

Table 6.5. Regression of DW-NOMINATE Scores on Party, Religion, and Controls, by Decade: House Models (clustered standard errors in parentheses)

	Model 1				Model 2			
	1970s	1980s	1990s	2000s	1970s	1980s	1990s	2000s
Member Characteristics								
Democrat	−0.574***	−0.649***	−0.752***	−0.837***				
	(−56.18)	(−50.70)	(−53.50)	(−64.64)				
Jewish					−0.113**	−0.172***	−0.227***	−0.274***
					(−2.74)	(−3.94)	(−4.86)	(−5.34)
Liberal Protestant					0.220***	0.150***	0.196***	0.273***
					(9.33)	(4.26)	(4.10)	(4.95)
Moderate Protestant					0.250***	0.176***	0.173***	0.190***
					(9.15)	(4.86)	(3.85)	(3.83)
Conservative Protestant					0.199***	0.142**	0.191***	0.245***
					(6.68)	(3.26)	(3.93)	(4.78)
Female								
Standardized District Characteristics								
Democratic President Vote Share								
African American Population								
Foreign-Born Population								
Blue-Collar Population								
Median Income of Population								
Constant	0.271	0.331	0.384	0.437	−0.233	−0.140	−0.114	−0.117
N	2515	2184	2166	2389	1895	2164	2110	2297
R-Squared	0.683	0.765	0.813	0.873	0.112	0.075	0.086	0.121

***$p < .001$, ** $p < .01$, * $p < .05$

	Model 3				Model 4			
	1970s	1980s	1990s	2000s	1970s	1980s	1990s	2000s
	−0.541***	−0.632***	−0.729***	−0.818***	−0.505***	−0.541***	−0.608***	−0.670***
	(−45.20)	(−48.23)	(−48.57)	(−58.01)	(−31.17)	(−41.87)	(−38.45)	(−48.62)
	−0.090***	−0.076**	−0.053*	−0.009	0.002	−0.026	−0.042*	0.001
	(−3.89)	(−3.13)	(−2.11)	(−0.41)	(0.06)	(−1.27)	(−1.99)	(0.05)
	0.082**	0.048**	0.053**	0.029	0.025	0.002	0.007	0.008
	(5.64)	(2.88)	(2.78)	(1.44)	(1.43)	(0.10)	(0.41)	(0.49)
	0.119***	0.091***	0.062**	0.053**	0.032	0.032	0.023	0.007
	(7.28)	(5.04)	(3.04)	(3.08)	(1.57)	(1.91)	(1.36)	(0.50)
	0.121***	0.064**	0.058**	0.052**	0.053*	0.044*	0.061**	0.047***
	(7.24)	(3.09)	(2.73)	(2.95)	(2.41)	(2.50)	(3.16)	(3.31)
					−0.030	−0.037	−0.028	
					(−1.14)	(−1.56)	(−1.23)	
					−0.061***	−0.121***	−0.111***	−0.112***
					(−7.38)	(−14.80)	(−11.23)	(−18.20)
					−0.015	0.023***	0.001	
					(−1.84)	(3.45)	(0.15)	
					−0.076***	−0.034***	−0.010**	
					(−6.74)	(−6.64)	(−2.76)	
					−0.009	−0.006	0.028**	
					(−0.95)	(−0.66)	(2.86)	
					−0.125**	−0.024*	0.018***	
					(−3.10)	(−2.19)	(3.49)	
	0.186	0.283	0.340	0.397	0.085	0.203	0.314	0.363
	1878	2156	2095	1870	783	1731	856	2297
	0.692	0.779	0.817	0.875	0.738	0.851	0.881	0.919

***$p < .001$, ** $p < .01$, * $p < .05$

or state leans Republican or Democratic. Canes-Wrone, Cogan, and Brady (2002), Ansolabehere, Snyder, and Stewart (2000), and Erickson and Wright (1980) use district-level presidential election returns as a proxy for district ideology (see Levendusky et al. [2008]). Additional controls are intended to account for other district- and state-level characteristics that might influence a member's ideological leaning based on accommodation to her or his constituency: size of the African American population, size of the foreign-born (as a proxy for immigrant) population, representation of blue-collar workers (in percentages), and median income. We expect that the impact of each of these factors will be to increase liberal voting among legislators. Our goal, then, is to examine whether religion's impact on ideology persists net of the influence of these control variables and of party.

Beginning with results for the House in table 6.5, the coefficients in model 1 show that party exerts a strong, negative effect on votes in every decade, with Democrats—as expected—significantly more liberal in their voting stance than Republicans. The importance of party affiliation in influencing ideology is clearly evident in the R-squared statistics at the bottom of the table. In the 1970s party alone accounted for fully 68.3 percent of the variance in ideology, a figure that increased steadily in each decade through the 2000s, when more than 87 percent of the variance in vote was explained by party affiliation. The importance of party in explaining congressional ideology over this time period cannot be overstated; indeed, the effect of party, already strong in the 1970s, became even stronger in each successive decade.

In model 2 in table 6.5, we remove party and fit a series of dummy variables for religion; Catholics are the reference group. Our purpose here is to assess the role of religion apart from party in shaping roll call voting ideology. Keeping in mind that negative Common Space scores reflect a more liberal, and positive scores a more conservative, voting pattern, the model coefficients show that, first, in every decade, only Jews voted more liberally than Catholics and, second, every Protestant group is more conservative in its voting than either Jews or Catholics. Among the three major Protestant groups, the pattern of the coefficients indicates that Conservative Protestants do not always display the most conservative voting patterns, however. In the earlier two decades, for instance, it was Moderate Protestants who were the most conservative ($b = .250$ in the 1970s and .176 in the 1980s). Liberal Protestants were the more conservative in the latter decades ($b = .196$ in the 1990s and .273 in the 2000s).

What shall we make of the seemingly counterintuitive finding that Conservative Protestants vote more rather than less liberally than other Protestant denominations? The explanation lies in the fact that black Protestants—who are conservative in theology though not in actual voting—are included in the

Conservative Protestant category and thus exert a liberalizing effect on this group's overall pattern of voting. As we shall see shortly, this trend continues with model 3 before reverting to the expected pattern in the full model. Taken alone—that is, without considering party—religion accounts for between 7.5 percent (in the 1980s) and 12.1 percent (in the 2000s) of the variance in voting ideology. Like party, the contribution of religion to explained variance in ideology has increased steadily since the 1980s, albeit much more modestly.

Model 3 in table 6.5 fits terms for both party and religion, and it yields several interesting findings. First, Conservative Protestants exhibited the most conservative voting pattern in the 1970s ($b = .121$); second, in every other decade it was Moderate Protestants who voted most conservatively (though the coefficients for Moderate and Conservative Protestants in the decade of the 2000s are nearly identical), again reflecting the presence of liberal-voting black Protestants among the ranks of Conservative Protestants; and third, increments to explained variance in ideology attributable to adding religion to the party-only model are quite modest in each decade. Nevertheless, only one of the religion coefficients in model 2 is not significant, indicating that religion does play a modest role in shaping ideology. Moreover, as a comparison of party coefficients in models 1 and 3 indicates, the inclusion of religion in the model moderates the magnitudes of the party coefficients in every decade, another indication of religion's impact on vote.

Finally, model 4 in table 6.5 adds to the previous model terms for the control variables. Net of the controls, Conservative Protestants are the most conservative of the religious groups in every decade; Jews and Catholics are the most liberal; and Liberal and Moderate Protestants are intermediate.

The model 4 coefficients that reflect the impact of the control variables on ideology reveal several noteworthy results. Though gender is not significant, in every decade[4] those representatives whose districts tended to vote Democrat in the previous presidential election were (not surprisingly) more liberal than those whose districts tended to vote Republican. Legislators from districts with larger proportions of African American constituents voted more conservatively in the 1980s; those whose constituents were more likely to be foreign-born voted more liberally in each decade; those from districts with a greater share of blue-collar workers voted more conservatively in the 1990s; in the 1970s and 1980s (but not in the 1990s), as median income increased, voting became more liberal; and in the 1990s the opposite pattern existed, with voting tending to be more conservative.

Table 6.6 displays results from regressing Common Space scores in the Senate on the same set of predictors that we used in the House. The baseline model 1 shows that party exerts a strong effect on vote, with Senate Democrats, like their House counterparts, significantly more liberal than Republicans

Table 6.6. Regression of DW-NOMINATE Scores on Party, Religion, and Controls, by Decade: Senate Models (clustered standard errors in parentheses)

	Model 1				Model 2			
	1970s	1980s	1990s	2000s	1970s	1980s	1990s	2000s
Member Characteristics								
Democrat	−0.568***	−0.632***	−0.674***	−0.710***				
	(−24.68)	(−24.94)	(−27.71)	(−30.52)				
Jewish					−0.026	0.004	−0.288**	−0.259**
					(−0.38)	(0.03)	(−2.99)	(−3.15)
Liberal Protestant					0.198***	0.099	0.159	0.151
					(3.47)	(1.25)	(1.79)	(1.76)
Moderate Protestant					0.091	0.049	0.089	0.066
					(1.44)	(0.51)	(0.86)	(0.69)
Conservative Protestant					0.146*	0.164	0.251*	0.289***
					(2.40)	(1.68)	(2.41)	(3.48)
Female								
Standardized District Characteristics								
Democratic President Vote Share								
African American Population								
Foreign-Born Population								
Blue-Collar Population								
Median Income of Population								
Constant	0.262	0.325	0.351	0.381	−0.191	−0.066	−0.067	−0.050
N	603	501	504	492	484	500	497	483
R-Squared	0.683	0.811	0.835	0.869	0.048	0.027	0.156	0.165

***$p < .001$, ** $p < .01$, * $p < .05$

	Model 3				Model 4			
	1970s	1980s	1990s	2000s	1970s	1980s	1990s	2000s
	−0.555***	−0.638***	−0.655***	−0.686***	−0.600***	−0.619***	−0.637***	−0.627***
	(−22.02)	(−26.53)	(−28.08)	(−28.21)	(−22.25)	(−27.31)	(−30.23)	(−24.44)
	−0.059	−0.035	−0.103*	−0.076	0.003	−0.034	−0.117*	−0.058
	(−0.83)	(−0.73)	(−2.11)	(−1.96)	(0.04)	(−0.72)	(−2.40)	(−1.64)
	0.032	−0.003	0.017	0.051	−0.013	−0.018	−0.017	0.024
	(1.16)	(−0.09)	(0.52)	(1.83)	(−0.42)	(−0.67)	(−0.59)	(0.96)
	0.050	0.091**	0.068*	0.044	0.011	0.045	0.017	0.004
	(1.59)	(2.78)	(2.01)	(1.43)	(0.33)	(1.64)	(0.54)	(0.17)
	0.044	0.065	0.065	0.074*	0.031	0.027	0.006	0.036
	(1.49)	(1.81)	(1.78)	(2.46)	(0.95)	(0.89)	(0.17)	(1.29)
					−0.060	−0.163***	−0.059	—
					(−1.95)	(−4.93)	(−1.54)	
					−0.057***	−0.175***	−0.127***	−0.104***
					(−3.94)	(−6.27)	(−4.90)	(−5.22)
					0.080***	0.070***	0.027	—
					(3.44)	(3.42)	(1.39)	
					−0.051	−0.009	−0.001	—
					(−1.17)	(−0.48)	(−0.03)	
					−0.035	−0.015	0.009	—
					(−1.77)	(−0.55)	(0.25)	
					−0.204	−0.053	0.038**	—
					(−1.96)	(−1.92)	(3.24)	
	0.222	0.301	0.320	0.342	0.100	0.208	0.317	0.330
	482	500	497	483	191	401	201	483
	0.684	0.826	0.855	0.888	0.798	0.883	0.894	0.912

***p < .001, ** p < .01, * p < .05

in every decade. With *R*-squared values increasing monotonically across the decades (from 68.3 percent of variance explained by party in the decade of the 1970s to 86.9 percent in the 2000s), the effect of party on ideology is as strong and consistent in the Senate as it is in the House.

In model 2 of table 6.6, we fit terms for religion only. As in the House, Jewish members of the Senate are the most liberal, followed by Catholics. Conservative Protestant legislators were the most conservative in every decade save for the 1970s, when they ranked second. Since there were so few African Americans in the Senate during the time period under study, Conservative Protestant voting patterns are not moderated by the presence of black Protestants as they were in the House.

In the Senate, *R*-squared statistics ranged from a low of 2.7 percent of variance explained in the 1980s to a high of 16.5 percent in the 2000s. As in the House, the proportion of variance in ideology that is attributable to religion has increased monotonically since the 1980s.

Model 3 fits terms for both party and religion. The coefficients reveal a strong and significant impact of party net of religion in every decade, with Democrats in the Senate consistently more liberal than Republicans. Few of the religion coefficients reach significance, though Conservative Protestant legislators remain more conservative in their voting patterns in the decade of the 2000s regardless of party affiliation ($b = .074$), and Moderate Protestants were the most conservative in the 1980s and 1990s.

Model 4 coefficients indicate that, over and above the effects of religion and of controls for the various member and district- or state-level characteristics, Democrats remained more liberal than Republicans in every decade. Moreover, religion rarely reached significance, and women legislators voted more liberally in the 1980s but not in other decades. The only control variables that shaped ideology were Democratic vote share in the previous presidential election, which led to more liberal voting in every decade; the proportion of African American members of Congress, which fostered more conservative voting in the 1970s and 1980s; and income, which yielded more conservative voting in the 1990s.

SUMMARY AND CONCLUSIONS

In earlier chapters, we focused attention on a targeted set of social issues in order to examine the nexus between religion and vote in Congress. In this chapter, we broadened our focus to include a measure that aggregates all roll call votes by chamber and member between 1969 and 2010 in an effort to determine if the impact of religion extends beyond such contentious issues as abortion, defense spending, taxes, and welfare. Our goal in this chapter was, first, to examine whether the religious affiliations of members of Congress are correlated with their overall voting behavior and, second, to determine if religion is implicated in the growing partisan polarization in Congress over the past four decades.

Our answer to both of these questions is *yes*. Although party affiliation remains the strongest predictor of voting behavior in models both with and without controls for other factors that might help to explain ideology, religion is also correlated in expected ways with voting behavior. These findings support other recent work on the determinants of congressional voting that has highlighted religion as one factor among many in contributing to the culture wars (see especially Asmussen 2011). Our analysis also shows that over the past four decades, members of Conservative Protestant religious denominations have increased their representation in the Republican Party while declining in number in the Democratic Party. We have argued that this influx of Conservative Protestant members into the ranks of the Republicans, and their simultaneous departure from the ranks of the Democrats, has contributed to polarization between the parties. Congressional scholars would do well to consider the role of religion in future studies of polarization.

The chapter began with two opposing views of the preferred connection between faith and politics. The next chapter turns attention squarely to polarization among the general public by examining the question whether—and if so to what extent—congressional voting behavior reflects trends in public attitudes.

7

Toeing the Party Line

The Increasing Influence of Partisanship among White Protestants and White Catholics, 1972–2010

Robert P. Jones and Daniel Cox

Other chapters in this volume have focused on the relative influence that religious affiliation and party affiliation have played over time among members of Congress.[1] The examination of roll call votes over the last four decades demonstrates that during the Reagan years, partisanship began to play an increasingly influential role and ultimately trumped religious affiliation as a predictor of key votes, especially on social issues such as abortion.

The task of this chapter is to examine whether and to what extent partisanship has trumped religious affiliation in predicting attitudes on important social questions among the general public, specifically among white Protestants and white Catholics. We proceed in three steps. First, we give a brief introduction demonstrating the shifting party identification among white Protestants and white Catholics between 1972 and 2010. Second, we examine to what extent partisan polarization has occurred among these two religious groups with respect to two social issues: abortion and the rights of gay and lesbian Americans. Finally, we conduct a series of regression models to determine the degree to which political partisanship has become an independent predictor of views on social issues, and we explore its relative strength over the last four decades.

Our analysis demonstrates that, like congressional leaders, white Protestants and white Catholics began polarizing on social issues in the 1980s during the Reagan presidency, and party affiliation began to play a stronger independent role in predicting views on these issues during this period. We also found, however, that polarization and the influence of partisanship affects white Protestants differently than white Catholics. Since the early 1990s, white Protestants have become politically polarized around both the issue of abortion and the morality of same-sex sexual relations, and party affiliation has played an increasingly strong role on both of these issues. In contrast, polarization among white Catholics has been, for the most part, limited to the morality of same-sex relationships; the independent influence of partisanship is largely seen in the area of gay and lesbian rights and much less so on abortion.

PARTY IDENTIFICATION AMONG
WHITE PROTESTANTS AND CATHOLICS (1972–2010)

Before delving into the deeper questions of polarization and the independent influence of partisanship, we begin with a brief overview of shifts in party identification among white Protestants and white Catholics between 1972 and 2010, which provides important context for the remainder of the analysis. In general, Democratic affiliation has seen a considerable decline among white Christians, with the most precipitous plunge in identification concentrated among white Catholics.

White Protestants

Beginning in the 1960s, southern whites, the majority of whom were Protestant, began shifting their political allegiances. Finding themselves frequently at odds with the Democratic Party over the party's embrace of civil rights, its stance on the ERA, and other sensitive cultural issues, they began to abandon the Democrats (Black and Black 2003).[2] This shift accelerated under President Reagan, who was enormously popular among southern whites. Between 1980, Reagan's first year in office, and 1989, Democratic affiliation among white Protestants fell nine points, from 46 percent to 37 percent. The Republican Party, which faced a eight-point deficit in party affiliation among white Protestants in 1980 (46 percent to 38 percent, respectively), claimed a twelve-point advantage among this important religious constituency nine years later (49 percent to 37 percent, respectively).

Democratic affiliation among white Protestants continued to drop through the 1990s (albeit more modestly), reaching a nadir of 30 percent in 2004. The Republican advantage hit its apex during this same period, with 55 percent of white Protestants identifying as Republican. In 2010, nearly half (49 percent) of white Protestants identified as Republicans, compared with roughly one-third (34 percent) who identified as Democrats.

White Catholics

A similar but even more dramatic drop in Democratic affiliation also occurred during the Reagan years, this time among white Catholics. In 1972, nearly two out of every three (65 percent) white Catholics identified with the Democratic Party, while only one in five (20 percent) identified as Republican. In 1978, more than six in ten (62 percent) white Catholics identified as Democrat, and 22 percent identified as Republican. Ten years later, as Reagan was completing his second term, less than half (48 percent) of white Catholics identified with the Democratic Party, and nearly four in ten (39 percent) identified with the GOP.

Unlike white Protestants, who saw modest partisan affiliation shifts after the Reagan era, the erosion of Democratic identity among white Catholics continued steadily over the next two decades. In 1990, the Democratic Party maintained a three-point advantage over the Republican Party among white Catholics (47 percent to 44 percent, respectively). In 2010, only one-third of white Catholics identified as Democrats, compared with 46 percent who identified as Republicans—a thirteen-point GOP advantage (General Social Survey 1972–2010).[3]

INCREASING POLARIZATION ON SOCIAL ISSUES AMONG WHITE PROTESTANTS AND WHITE CATHOLICS (1972–2010)

Scholars of public opinion and political science have spilled much ink over the concept of political polarization, beginning with a debate over its existence and expanding into disputes over polarization's causes and consequences. There is a general scholarly consensus that congressional polarization is, in fact, real (Brady and Han 2006; Fleisher and Bond 2004; Jacobson 2003; Poole and Rosenthal 1984). But there is more disagreement about whether—and to what degree—polarization is occurring among the general public, as well as how polarization should be defined. For example, Fiorina et al. argue that at the ballot box, voters are forced to make more polarized choices but are nevertheless moderate in their ideological disposition. Abramowitz and Saunders, on the other hand, make the case that increased ideological consistency in the views of the mass public is evidence of polarization (Abramowitz and Saunders 2008; Fiorina, Abrams, and Pope 2005). Hetherington suggests that the discrepancy in the findings is the result of how the concept of polarization is defined—"much of the disagreement can be understood as a question of definition" (Hetherington 2009, 415).

In this volume, polarization has been shown to exist at the congressional level, where partisan attachment has preempted religious affiliation as a guiding influence on political behavior. What remains to be answered, however, is whether—and to what degree—polarization has occurred among the rank-and-file members of specific religious communities.[4] To answer this question, we analyze two major religious groups, white Protestants and white

Catholics, and their views on two controversial social issues, the legality of abortion and gay and lesbian issues.

On important social and cultural questions like abortion as well as gay and lesbian issues, white Catholics' and white Protestants' views diverge along political lines: white Catholic Democrats closely align with Democrats overall, while white Protestant Republicans closely align with Republicans overall. On some issues such as abortion, the divergence has been dramatic, while on others it has been more modest. Overall, this apparent political polarization is generally greater among white Protestants than among white Catholics (General Social Survey 1972–2010).

Polarization on Abortion

Among the many culture war issues, abortion is a common hub for strong, polarizing attitudes. It is a paragon of Carmines and Stimson's "easy" issue, a topic on which Americans are able to render considered judgments without much technical expertise (Carmines and Stimson 1980).

Among the general public, views on abortion have remained remarkably stable over the last thirty years. In 1980, 53 percent of the public agreed that abortion should be legal, while 43 percent said that the law should only permit abortions in certain circumstances or not at all. In 2008, 58 percent of the public agreed that the law should generally permit legal abortion, while 42 percent remained opposed.

However, Democrats' and Republicans' views on abortion have become remarkably polarized over this same period. Throughout the 1980s, there were few differences between the views of self-identified Democrats and Republicans on abortion policy: majorities of both groups favored legal abortion. This, however, began to shift in the early 1990s. By 2008, 62 percent of Democrats said that abortion should be legal compared with 49 percent of Republicans.

As the data presented in chapter 4 show, there is evidence that the issue of abortion actually altered Americans' partisan attachments (Adams 1997). Adams suggests that congressional polarization, as measured by congressional voting behavior,[5] influenced committed partisans to embrace each party's particular stance on abortion. As these divides crystallized, Democrats become the pro-choice party and Republicans become the pro-life party, a phenomenon known as "issue ownership" (Petrocik 1996). Several other studies have also shown that partisanship and abortion have become increasingly linked (Jelen 1997; Wilcox 2001).[6] In the following section, we demonstrate that both white Protestants and white Catholics have become increasingly polarized by partisanship on the issue of abortion.

White Protestants: Major Partisan Polarization on Abortion

Even nearly a decade after the *Roe v. Wade* decision legalized abortion, white Protestants' views on abortion did not differ appreciably from those of the general public. As figure 7.1 shows, in the early 1980s, a majority of the public and a similar majority of white Protestants said that abortion should be permitted (55 percent and 53 percent, respectively). During the following decades, support among white Protestants for legal abortion dropped modestly, with less than half (48 percent) of white Protestants currently saying that abortion should be legally permitted.

Throughout the 1980s, the differences between the views of white Protestant Democrats and Republicans on the issue of abortion were modest; on average, there was only a six-point difference. Over the next decade and into the twenty-first century, however, white Protestants who affiliated with the Democratic Party diverged strikingly from their co-religionists in the Republican Party. In 1988, there was only a five-point gap between white Protestant Democrats and Republicans, with at least half of each group reporting that abortion should be permitted (55 percent vs. 50 percent, respectively). By 2008, 69 percent of white Protestant Democrats reported supporting legal abortion, while 36 percent of white Protestant Republicans supported legal abortion. To put it simply, the partisan gap among white Protestants grew from only five points in 1988 to thirty-three points in 2008. This intragroup polarization among white Protestants is even greater than the partisan gap between Republicans and Democrats overall.

On this issue, white Protestant Democrats and white Protestant Republicans are not equally polarized. Rather, white Protestant Democrats' views differ increasingly from white Protestants overall, while white Protestant

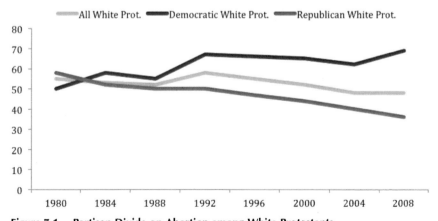

Figure 7.1. Partisan Divide on Abortion among White Protestants

Republicans remain more ideologically similar to white Protestants overall. As of 2008, less than half (48 percent) of white Protestants believed that abortion should be generally available, compared to 36 percent of white Protestant Republicans and 69 percent of white Protestant Democrats.

Sullins (1999) suggests that on the issue of abortion, views at the extreme are more important than the mean attitudes. If we examine views at the poles—focusing only on those who say that by law, a woman should always be able to obtain an abortion—the degree of polarization among white Protestants is even greater. Moreover, as figure 7.2 illustrates, the pattern of polarization is steady and the growth of partisan difference is linear. In 1980, an equal number of white Protestant Democrats and white Protestant Republicans agreed that women should always be able to obtain an abortion (33 percent). Over the next decade, the partisan gap shifted slightly but remained modest. By 1992, however, there was a sixteen-point gap between white Protestant Democrats and white Protestant Republicans: 50 percent and 34 percent, respectively. This partisan gap grew to a twenty-eight-point difference by 2008, when white Protestant Democrats were more than twice as likely as white Protestant Republicans to say that by law a woman should always be able to obtain an abortion (48 percent to 20 percent).

White Catholics: Modest Partisan Polarization on Abortion

In the early 1980s, White Catholics were significantly less supportive of legal abortion than were white Protestants. Less than half (45 percent) of white Catholics said that abortion should be legally permitted in cases other than the situations of rape, incest, or threat to the mother's life. Over the next

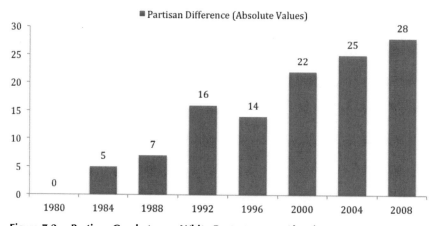

Figure 7.2.   **Partisan Gap between White Protestants on Abortion**

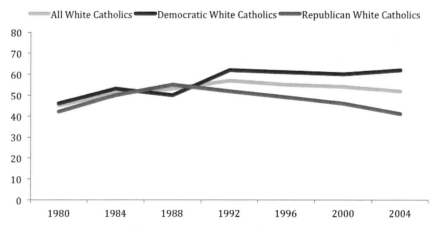

Figure 7.3. **Partisan Divide on Abortion among White Catholics**

decade, support for legalized abortion increased to majority territory, where it has remained ever since. In 2004, a slim majority (52 percent) of white Catholics said that abortion should be legally permitted.[7]

Like white Protestants, white Catholics exhibit similar patterns of polarization on the issue of abortion, although the degree of polarization is more modest. As figure 7.3 displays, in 1980 similar numbers of white Catholic Democrats (46 percent) and white Catholic Republicans (42 percent) believed that abortion should be legally permitted either always or in cases other than the situations of rape, incest, or threat to the life of the mother. By 1992, a ten-point gap opened in views about the legality of abortion between white

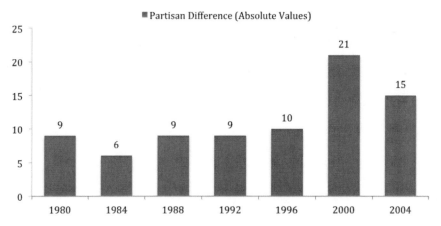

Figure 7.4. **Partisan Gap between White Catholics on Abortion**

Catholic Democrats and white Catholic Republicans (62 percent and 52 percent, respectively). This gap increased to more than twenty points by 2004, when 62 percent of white Catholic Democrats and only 41 percent of white Catholic Republicans affirmed the legality of abortion. Unlike the pattern among white Protestants, the polarization between white Catholic Republicans and Democrats was relatively even.

At the poles, the differences between Republican and white Catholic Democrats also increased, albeit much more modestly than among white Protestants. Unlike white Protestants, who became polarized during the 1980s and 1990s, by 1980 white Catholics were already somewhat polarized around the issue of abortion, as shown in figure 7.4. In 1980, 20 percent of white Catholic Republicans and 29 percent of white Catholic Democrats affirmed the statement that "by law a woman should always be able to obtain an abortion." This difference increased to twenty-one points in 2000 before contracting slightly to a fifteen-point difference in 2004.[8]

Polarization in Views of Gay and Lesbian People and Same-Sex Relationships

In addition to abortion, one of the central fronts of the culture wars has been fought over expanding rights for gay and lesbian people. Americans' attitudes toward gay and lesbian people and their comfort with same-sex relationships have undergone a sea change over the last thirty years. Across every demographic group, there is evidence of an upsurge in positive views about gay and lesbian people, increased support for policies associated with gay and lesbian people (Brewer and Wilcox 2005), and greater acceptance of homosexuality (Yang 1997).

Like abortion, there is evidence of polarization among the general public on the issue of same-sex marriage (Abramowitz and Saunders 2008), and there is anecdotal evidence that the issue is also creating divisions within particular denominations (Dewan 2011; Nakamura 2011). In this section we demonstrate that, like abortion, attitudes about gay and lesbian people have become increasingly polarized along party lines among white Catholics and white Protestants.

White Protestants: Major Partisan Polarization
on Views of Gay and Lesbian People and Attitudes
about Morality of Same-Gender Sexual Relations

Like those of the general public, white Protestant attitudes toward gay and lesbian people have evolved significantly from the early 1980s. In 1984, on a one-hundred-point feeling thermometer scale (in which one hundred represents feeling very warmly toward a group and zero represents feeling very coldly toward a group), white Protestants' average feeling toward gay and lesbian people was 23.6. As the illustrated feeling thermometer in figure 7.5 depicts, the differences between white Protestant Democrats and white Protestant Republicans were slim (26.9 to 21.6, respectively). By 1992, however, white Protestant Democrats had begun to evince warmer feelings toward gay and lesbian people (38.2 percent) than white Protestant Republicans (29 percent). And by 2004, the gap between white Protestant Democrats (56 percent) and white Protestant Republicans (39 percent) had grown to eighteen points.

Views about the morality of sexual relations between same-sex couples were also subject to significant polarization among white Protestants. In the early 1970s, strong majorities of both the general public and white Protestants agreed that sex between people of the same gender was always wrong, including 79 percent of white Protestant Democrats and 77 percent of white Protestant Republicans. As figure 7.6 shows, views remained relatively stable over the next two decades; from 1973 to 1987 there was on average only a three-point difference between the views of white Protestant Democrats and Republicans.

During the 1990s, however, the average distance between the views of white Protestant Democrats and Republicans increased significantly. The average distance between white Protestant Democrats and Republicans more than tripled from three points to eleven points over the next decade (1988–1998). The average distance between the two groups then doubled during the following decade (2000–2010), accelerating from an eleven-point

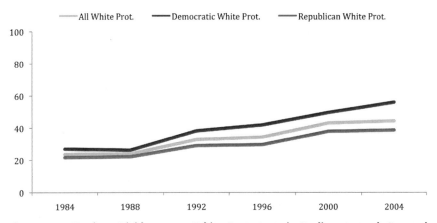

Figure 7.5. Partisan Divide among White Protestants in Feelings toward Gay and Lesbian People

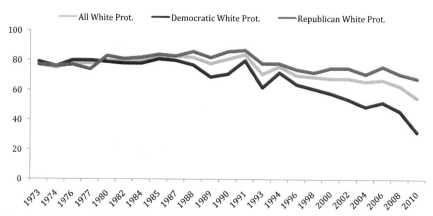

Figure 7.6. Partisan Divide among White Protestants in Attitudes about Same-Sex Sexual Relationships

average difference to a twenty-four-point average difference. By 2010, the gap between white Protestant Democrats and Republicans had grown to thirty-six points; less than one-third (32 percent) of white Protestant Democrats believed that sex between two adults of the same gender was always wrong, compared with more than two-thirds (68 percent) of white Protestant Republicans.

The growing partisan divide among white Protestants is primarily the result of shifts occurring among white Protestant Democrats. Over the last forty years, views of white Protestant Republicans have remained relatively stable, falling only slightly over the last two decades. In 1973, 77 percent of white Protestant Republicans said that sex between two people of the same gender was always wrong; in 2010, that number had fallen only to 68 percent. Among white Protestant Democrats, however, the change in attitudes about the morality of same-gender sexual relationships has been dramatic. In 1973, 79 percent white Protestant Democrats said same-gender sex was wrong; by 2010, only 32 percent embraced this view, a forty-seven-point shift.

White Catholics: Modest Partisan Polarization
on Views of Gay and Lesbian People and Attitudes
about Morality of Same-Gender Sexual Relations

The pattern for Catholics, once again, shows more modest partisan polarization than among Protestants. There is, for example, little evidence of increasing polarization on attitudes about gay and lesbian people through the 1980s and 1990s. Views of white Catholic Democrats and Republicans diverged between 1984 and 1988, as figure 7.7 shows, but these differences remained relatively constant as the two groups' positive feelings toward gay and lesbian people increased in tandem through 2004.

In 1984, the average feeling thermometer rating among white Catholic Democrats toward gay and lesbian people was 35.4 compared to 36.7 for white Catholic Republicans. In 1988, views diverged modestly to an average score of 38.7 for white Catholic Democrats and 31.3 for white Catholic Republicans, a 7.4-point difference, which remained constant over the next decade and a half. By 2004, both groups' positive feelings toward gay and lesbian people increased significantly, with white Catholic Democrats reporting an average feeling score of 57.2 and white Catholic Republicans reporting a score of 50.2. The average distance between white Catholic Democrats and Republicans in 2004 was, at seven points, essentially unchanged from 1988.

The data on attitudes about sex between two adults of the same gender paint a similar portrait. Figure 7.8 illustrates that prior to 1994, the differences between the views of white Catholic Democrats and Republicans were negligible; the absolute average distance between the views of white Catholic Democrats and Republicans was only 4 percentage points. In 1994, there was a slightly larger gap, with 58 percent of white Catholic Democrats and 64 percent of white Catholic Republicans saying that sex between people of the same gender is always wrong. Nearly a decade later, though, the percentage of white Catholic Democrats who agreed that sex between adults of the same gender is always wrong had dropped precipitously, while the decline among white Catholic Republicans was less dramatic. In 2010, the number had

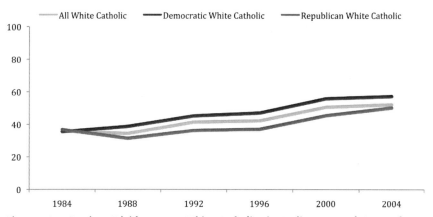

Figure 7.7. Partisan Divide among White Catholics in Feelings toward Gay and Lesbian People

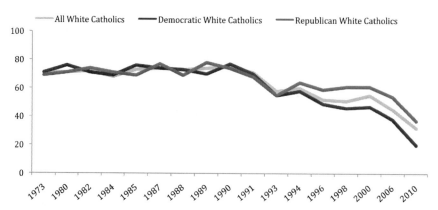

Figure 7.8. Partisan Divide among White Catholics in Attitudes about Same-Sex Sexual Relations

dropped to 20 percent of white Catholic Democrats and 37 percent of white Catholic Republicans, a seventeen-point gap.

THE INCREASING PREDICTIVE POWER OF PARTY AFFILIATION IN VIEWS ABOUT LEGAL ABORTION AND THE MORALITY OF SAME-SEX SEXUAL RELATIONS

In order to investigate whether the relative strength of party affiliation has increased as a predictor of attitudes on these social issues, we measured the independent influence of partisanship while holding constant other demographic characteristics (e.g., education, age, gender, region, and frequency of worship attendance) among both white Protestants and white Catholics. The full logistic regression output, on which the following discussion is based, is available in appendix B.

White Protestants, Party Affiliation, and Attitudes about Abortion

In 1980, among white Protestants, Democratic affiliation predicted greater *opposition* to legalized abortion, while Republican affiliation was not a significant predictor of abortion attitudes. By 1990, Democratic partisan affiliation became a significant predictor of *support* for legalized abortion, while Republican affiliation remained an insignificant predictor. The predictive power of Democratic affiliation increased marginally by 2000, although college education and weekly worship attendance exhibited significantly stronger predictive power in both 1990 and 2000.

By 2008, Democratic affiliation had become the strongest predictor of attitudes about abortion: White Protestant Democrats were twice as likely as white Protestant independents to believe that abortion should be legal. In 2008, Republican affiliation was, for the first time, also a significant predictor of opposition to legal abortion among white Protestants, although it was only marginally significant ($p < .10$). Education and religious attendance were also significant predictors of white Protestants' views on abortion. White Protestants with a college education were less likely than those without a college education to say abortion should be illegal in most or all circumstances, while those who attended religious services at least once a week were about twice as likely to say that abortion should be illegal in most or all circumstances, compared with those who attended religious services less frequently.

These findings strengthen our observations of polarization discussed previously. Democratic Party affiliation not only increased in power as an independent predictor of attitudes on abortion during this period but also changed direction. In 1980, Democratic affiliation predicted opposition to legal abortion among white Protestants. By 1990, it predicted support for legal abortion, and the independent predictive power of party affiliation grew significantly from 1990 to 2008.

White Protestants, Party Affiliation, and Attitudes about the Morality of Same-Sex Relationships

Party affiliation is also becoming a stronger predictor of views about the morality of same-sex sexual relations. In 1980, neither Democratic nor Republican identity predicted attitudes about the morality of same-sex sexual relations. By 1990, Democratic affiliation exhibited a significant but modest impact; compared with white Protestant Democrats, white Protestant independents were about 1.5 times as likely to believe sexual relations between adults of the same gender was always wrong.

In 2000, Democratic affiliation was not a significant predictor, while Republican affiliation was only a marginally significant predictor. In 2010, however, Democratic affiliation far and away exhibited the strongest influence in attitudes about the morality of same-sex sexual relations. In 2010, white Protestant Democrats were more than three times as likely as white Protestant independents to view same-sex sexual relations as morally acceptable.

White Catholics, Party Affiliation, and Attitudes about Abortion

Across the four different years we analyzed, party affiliation was a significant predictor of attitudes on abortion among white Catholics only in 1990 and 2010. In 1990, white Catholic Democrats were more likely to support legalized abortion than were independents, but the effect was only marginally significant ($p < .10$). In 2010, Democratic affiliation was not a significant predictor of attitudes on abortion. White Catholic Republicans were significantly less likely to favor legal abortion, but here also the effect was only marginally significant ($p < .10$).

White Catholics, Party Affiliation, and Attitudes about Same-Sex Relationships

In 1980 and 1990, party affiliation had no discernible impact on white Catholics' views of the morality of same-sex sexual relations. However, in 2000, Democratic affiliation emerged as a significant predictor of views about the morality of sex between people of the same gender. In fact, in 2000, partisan attachment exhibited a stronger effect than any other factor in the model. In 2010, the impact of Democratic Party affiliation among Catholics was even larger than in 2000, although the effect was smaller than college education or frequency of worship attendance.

In conclusion, although white Catholics exhibited modest polarization on social issues when other demographic characteristics were controlled for, Democratic Party affiliation has a significant and increasingly large impact on attitudes toward the morality of same-sex sexual relations but not on abortion.

These more muted findings among white Catholics could be the result of two factors. First, compared to white Protestants, white Catholics exhibited more modest political polarization overall on both abortion and gay and lesbian issues. Thus, the lower levels of significance of party affiliation in the regression models likely reflect this more modest polarization. Second, the white Catholic analysis was conducted on a much smaller sample size than the analysis of white Protestants, which may have prevented effects from reaching statistical significance.

CONCLUSION

The results of this analysis strongly suggest that polarization is occurring among white Christians on social issues. The degree of polarization, the issues around which groups are polarized, and the relative impact of party affiliation, however, differ significantly between white Protestants and white Catholics.

Since the early 1990s, white Protestants have become politically polarized around both the issue of abortion and the morality of same-sex sexual relations. The regression models confirm that this polarization is driven particularly by Democratic Party affiliation, which has become a stronger predictor over time of attitudes about both abortion and the morality of same-sex relationships.

The picture among white Catholics is more complex. Polarization among white Catholics has been more focused, occurring primarily on the morality of same-sex sexual relations and much less so on the issue of abortion. The regression models confirm that partisanship is playing only a marginally significant role on the issue of abortion; although partisanship plays a more significant role on the issue of the morality of same-sex relationships, it is less significant than other factors such as education, age, gender, and frequency of religious attendance. Frequency of attendance has become increasingly important among white Catholics in predicting attitudes about abortion and gay and lesbian issues, lending some support for Hunter's (1991) hypothesis that, particularly on social issues, the dividing lines may be deepening between white Catholics who are more closely connected to churches and those with more tenuous connections.

The data on polarization and the regression models also suggest that we can expect that gay and lesbian issues, particularly the issue of same-sex marriage, will be an issue around which religious groups will become increasingly polarized. The mutually reinforcing polarization among Democratic leaders and partisans who are increasingly supportive of same-sex relationships, and Republican leaders and partisans who remain staunchly opposed, seems likely to continue to fuel polarization and strengthen the effect of partisanship within religious groups.

8

Discussion and Conclusion

Our study began with a series of questions focusing on James Davison Hunter's 1991 and 1994 books on the culture wars. Hunter wrote about two distinct visions of the good society that he saw emerging. The orthodox vision was grounded in the belief in a transcendent God who created the world in seven days and provided a book (e.g., the Torah, the Bible, the Quran) that contains all the knowledge human beings needed in order to know, understand, and obey God's laws. In one such vision, Jesus Christ is understood to be one with God, the personal savior who leads all those who believe in Him to eternal salvation.

The progressive vision of the good society is grounded in the Enlightenment. While not denying the existence of a God or Divine Force that brought the world into being, this vision focuses on the human capacity to seek truth through reason and faith in all facets of our lives. For religious believers in this vision, human beings are endowed with both reason and faith and acknowledge the legitimacy of scientific thought. In the first vision, truth is known through books such as the Bible and needs only to be learned and obeyed, especially with regard to matters of sexuality and family. In the second vision, truth is sought through reason and faith. A major task is to distinguish between them.

In the years following the publication of Hunter's books, many social scientists questioned Hunter's conclusions, citing research that showed that only a minority of Americans were at either of the extremes; indeed, the center seemed as solid as it had been twenty years earlier. We cited several of these works in chapter 1, especially the study by DiMaggio, Evans, and Bryson (1996), which showed the center still holding on a wide range of issues, including abortion. These authors demonstrated that only a minority of respondents to a national survey was opposed to abortion under all circumstances, with the majority supporting abortion rights under some or most conditions. That would hardly suggest a culture war brewing. But DiMaggio et al. also noted that people who identified with either political party were deeply polarized over abortion. Were they an example of the Orthodox versus Progressive mix of Protestants, Catholics, Jews, and others? Might the religion of members of Congress then constitute a potent influence on voting in regard to issues such as abortion? Hunter had identified orthodox Catholics as those who accepted and followed the formal teaching of the Catholic Church in opposition to abortion under any and all circumstances. Progressive Catholics in Congress might be expected to cast their votes in accord with the Church's admonition to follow their consciences, which might or might not reflect the official Church teaching on abortion.[1] How would members of other religious groups vote on matters like abortion in Congress, whatever their religions' teachings?

Our focus throughout was on evidence that would either support or refute Hunter's hypothesis about the two visions as found in congressional roll call voting. Thus, we examined all abortion roll call votes from the 1977–1978 congressional session through the final vote on the health care bill in March 2010. We also tracked roll call votes on three of the issues that most frequently came before Congress during this period—defense spending, taxes, and welfare spending. Finally, we summarized fourteen other sets of key roll call votes in the House and Senate during the period 1969–2008 (see the link to appendix A). In each case, we examined both party and religious affiliation of House and Senate members. We separated votes by chamber for three reasons: (1) the two chambers do not always vote on the same issues in the same session; (2) the bills voted on do not always conform across chambers; and (3) at least in some historical periods, senators seemed to have been under less pressure to vote along party lines on issues like abortion and taxes than House members whose voting public is more local and who are subject to reelection every two years.

In chapter 2 we provided a brief overview of the beliefs, values, and practices of the major religious denominations in Congress since 1959, noting especially their pervasive influence on American culture. Their legacy includes an orthodoxy that sees America as blessed by God, mixed with a strong sense of personal autonomy. The other vision provides a progressive understanding of life that respects the difference between science and religion. Catholics and Jews made their particular adjustments to this legacy. A brief review of roll call voting patterns in Congress showed how changes in the religious makeup of the House and Senate influenced votes.

Chapter 3 described these compositional changes from 1959 to 2010. For example, in 1959 Mainline Protestants held 57 percent of seats in the House and 64 percent of the Senate. By the 111th Congress (2009–2010), their numbers had dropped to 34 percent in the House and 38 percent in the Senate.

Who were the beneficiaries of the declining representation of Mainline Protestants? As chapter 3 chronicles, the largest beneficiaries were Catholics in both parties, and Jews and blacks primarily in the Democratic Party. Catholics have become the largest single denomination in the country, with about 24 percent identifying with the Catholic Church. There were ninety Catholics holding seats in the House in 1959–1960 (seventy-six Democrats and fourteen Republicans). Their numbers increased slowly in the ensuing six decades, reaching a total of 133 in the 111th Congress (2009–2010), when Democrats reached a new high of ninety-four. In the five decades since 1959, Republican Catholics in the House more than doubled their numbers, with thirty-nine in the 111th Congress. During that time they have grown more rapidly than their Democratic co-religionists. Overall, Catholics held 30 percent of the House seats in 2009–2010.

Catholics also increased their numbers in the Senate. In 1959, all twelve Catholics in the Senate were Democrats. In the ensuing decades, Republican Catholics increased their numbers as high as thirteen; the number in 2009 was nine. In that same Congress, Catholic Democrats held sixteen seats, a new high. Altogether, Catholics held 25 percent of the Senate in 2009–2010, just about equal to their representation in the national population.

In 1959, Conservative Protestants held fifty-six seats in the House, including forty that were held by Southern Democrats. By 2009, there were only a few such Democrats left in the white Conservative Protestant group; many of the "new" so-called Conservative Protestants were African Americans, many from Southern states. Meanwhile, the number of Conservative Protestant Republicans more than doubled. Overall, they increased their numbers by about one-third, holding nineteen more seats in 2009 than in 1959.

The final notable beneficiaries of the changes since 1959 were Jews. Although Jews constitute only about 2 percent of the American population, they increased their numbers in the House from a total of ten (one Republican and nine Democrats) to thirty-two in the 111th Congress (only one a Republican). In 1979 and again in 1989, there were as many as five Republican Jews in the House. Thus, while the number of Jewish Democrats in the House tripled, the Republicans held only one seat in 2009–2010. In the Senate, Jews held two seats in 1959, one by a Republican and one by a Democrat. In the ensuing decades, Jewish Democrats reached a new high of ten, with no Republicans present. Senator Joseph Lieberman of Connecticut was registered as an independent, as was Senator Sanders of Vermont. Both caucused with the Democrats. In summary, in the Senate between 1959 and 2009, Mainline Protestants lost more than twenty seats while Catholics and Jews gained more than twenty, and Conservative Protestants gained nineteen.

The figures in chapter 3 showed that, over time, there has been a small but discernible move from Mainline Protestants to Catholics and Jews in the Senate and to Catholics, Jews, and Black Protestants in the House. The white Conservative Protestant Democrats in the House have been replaced by black Moderate and Progressive Democrats; on the Republican side, Conservative Protestant Republicans have more than doubled in numbers. Whether abortion was or is the exemplar of polarization in regard to congressional voting since the 1970s, unquestionably, religion has played a major role in the abortion issue. As Luker (1984) and others have documented, soon after *Roe v. Wade* became law (1973), Catholic groups formed to protest and attempt to minimize its impact. As noted in chapter 4, the Catholic bishops tried in vain to get candidate Carter and then-president Ford to adopt a platform plank outlawing abortion. Beginning in 1977, key Evangelical leaders started to convince Reagan to join their cause. As a consequence, Reagan was later able to convert Evangelicals to join, or at least to vote for, the Republican Party with promises of a stronger military, lower taxes, and an anti-abortion plank. In the years leading up to 1980, neither party had an exclusive pro-choice or pro-life stance. Catholic Democrats in both the House and the Senate were generally more pro-life before Reagan. In fact, the Republican-led Senate was strongly pro-choice during the first years of the Reagan administration. However, during the 1980s, Republican support for abortion rights decreased dramatically, from 70 percent (1980) to 48 percent (1988) and below 10 percent since 2004.

Changes in the number and location of Mainline Protestants also affected the abortion debate. For example, there were forty-one Mainline Protestant Republicans, more than 70 percent of whom were pro-choice (only nine of these were from Southern states). As the pro-life vote rose to 90 percent, there were only twenty-two Mainline Protestant Republicans, thirteen from Southern states.

In the early years following *Roe v. Wade*, Catholic Democrats in the House and Senate had been more pro-life than pro-choice, but as Republicans became more pro-life, Catholic Democrats became increasingly pro-choice (as figures 4.3a and 4.4a showed). In the House, there has been a consistent pro-life Catholic Democratic minority ranging from 35 to 20 percent since the 102nd Congress (1991–1992). There was no comparable small group of pro-choice members in the Republican House or Senate. Most Democrats also supported at least some of the bishops' social justice teachings. There were no Republicans in the House or Senate whose voting patterns approached anything close to a consistent ethic of life. Congressional Jews have been strong supporters of the pro-choice position since *Roe v. Wade*, which is not surprising due to the Jewish tradition of prioritizing the interests of the mother in most situations (with the exception of Orthodox and some Conservative Jews). Black Protestants in the House have also been almost 100 percent pro-choice, despite the strongly pro-life theology of black Protestant churches.

Thus, among Democrats, the overall picture has been one of religion playing a central role in the abortion debate. Among Republicans, on the other hand, party trumped religion on the issue of abortion. A closer look suggests that religious conservatives gradually increased their influence within the Republican Party in Congress as they replaced moderate with pro-life candidates. This influence was also evident among Republican party members in the general public.

In chapter 5 we addressed two questions. First, did polarization on abortion as observed in the House and Senate resurface in votes on any of the three key issues (defense, taxes, and welfare), and, if so, to what extent? Second, did religion influence votes on those three issues? We selected defense spending, taxes, and welfare spending because these three issues were voted on more frequently than most of the other issues that we identified from Barone's key roll call votes between 1969 and 2008. Furthermore, we saw these issues as important indicators of the distinctive visions of the good society held by the two parties. Republicans were expected to be stronger supporters of defense spending and traditional family values but opposed to tax increases and welfare spending. Democrats were expected to hold mixed views on defense spending, to be less supportive of tax cuts, and to be more in favor of welfare legislation. Regarding these three issues, polarization was clearly evident as early as 1983, with votes ranging as high as the 80–90 percent levels. By the mid-1990s, Republican votes begin to yield over 90 percent support for the party position.

Figures 5.1–5.5 showed the votes on defense spending. On several occasions, Mainline Protestant Republicans voted differently than the party as a whole. For example, during the latter part of the Reagan administration, H.R. 1748, 1987 (a vote to ban chemical weapons), and H.R. 444, 1988 (a vote to aid the Contras in Nicaragua), revealed a much lower level of support than the vote of the party as a whole. Catholics, especially Catholic Democrats, were the ones most likely to vote differently than the party as a whole, giving less support to the Vietnam War and, during the Reagan years, opposing Reagan's support for the Contras (H.R. 2760) and for continuing nerve gas production (H.R. 6030). In the Senate, we cited the example of the Mainline Protestant Democrats' votes in the period between 1981 and 1990. They were more likely than the Democratic Party overall to support President Reagan's

Cold War spending initiatives. On the other hand, Catholic Democrats during this same period gave virtually no support to Reagan's defense spending bills.

The Catholic bishops had written a pastoral letter, *The Challenge of Peace* (1983), that condemned nuclear weapons, nerve gas, and related weapons, as well as war in general. Catholic Democrats were more affected by the religious factor with an even lower proportion in favor of defense spending than Democrats as a whole. Thus, much of the legislation proposed by the Reagan administration was opposed by the bishops, and there was at least an association between the bishops' opposition and the votes of Catholic Democrats. On the other hand, Catholic Republicans strongly supported the party position through the Reagan years and into the twenty-first century. The patterns on tax cuts in the House and Senate were fairly similar, with more interparty support through 1986 and clear-cut polarization thereafter, especially within the House, which had almost consistent 100 percent support for tax cuts. This pattern of complete partisan opposition to taxes is best reflected by the fact that almost all Republicans signed on to Grover Norquist's "No Taxes" pledge (2008).

The one tax bill with bipartisan support was the 1986 bill authored by Representative Dan Rostenkowski (D-IL) and Senator Bill Packwood (R-OR). Catholic Democrats and Republicans in the House outvoted their parties by twenty points in support of this bill. The bill is unusual because it is the only time within our study period that Democrats agreed in significant numbers to reduce the marginal income tax rate. This was done as part of the compromise to eliminate many loopholes and deductions in the tax code that had generally benefited business owners. The bill also helped many higher-wage earners who lived in high-cost areas. The third key vote in this trilogy also reflected the two parties' distinctive visions about the good society as seen through its legislation. This was an area that Democrats have long sought to prioritize (Social Security, the G.I. Bill, Medicare, Medicaid, school lunch programs, Head Start, etc.). Several pieces of legislation on welfare bills revealed distinctive patterns among Catholics and Mainline Protestants in the Senate. For example, figures 5.21–5.23 showed that while Mainline Protestants, both Democrats and Republicans, occasionally strayed from their party positions through the mid- to late 1980s, polarization grew after that. Similarly, Catholic Democrats and Republicans were not generally polarized over welfare until 2000, after which party polarization also took over.

In sum, we found that polarizing tendencies became apparent during the Reagan administration, dipped a bit during the Clinton administration, and became strong in both parties in the George W. Bush administration. We have cited a number of situations where one or another group of House and Senate members who had identified themselves as Catholics or Mainline Protestants did in fact vote differently from their party, occasionally making a statement, if not a difference. The consequences were not as significant as with the votes on abortion legislation, but they do show that there is or can be a religious factor in the votes of House and Senate members.

In chapter 6 we examined the role of religion in Congress by analyzing all House and Senate votes between 1969 and 2010 rather than focusing only on the issues of abortion, defense spending, taxes, and welfare. We asked whether the polarization that was documented in earlier chapters was evident when all congressional votes were analyzed. Analysis of Poole's Common Space NOMINATE scores measuring ideology of legislators across all roll call votes showed clearly that Catholics and Jews have been the most liberal in their voting ideology during the period under study, followed (variously) by Liberal, Moderate, and Conservative Protestants. Without party in the model, religion explained between 7.5 and 12.1 percent of the variance in House voting and between 2.7 and 16.5 percent in Senate voting. We argued that the departure of Conservative Protestants from the ranks of the Democratic Party in favor of the Republican Party was very likely a major contributing factor to the polarization in Congress since the mid- to late 1970s.

Chapter 7 took us back to public opinion surveys and provided powerful support for the finding by DiMaggio et al. that one area in which measurable polarization in public opinion exists is abortion. Jones and Cox showed that the polarization in public opinion across parties was slower to materialize than the polarization in Congress itself beginning in the 1980s (see chapter 4). They found pro-life and pro-choice polarization in public opinion taking place in the 1990s, almost a decade later. Thus, while Jones and Cox found only a five-point gap between pro-life and pro-choice Protestant Republicans in 1988, in the House the gap was already 80 to 20 percent. House Republicans never approached 30 percent pro-choice. The gap was not as large in the Senate (see figures 4.1 and 4.2). Catholic Democrats always had a larger percentage of pro-life members in the House and Senate, reflecting the Jones and Cox findings among Catholics in public opinion polling. These findings lend support to Adams's (1997) argument that it was polarization in Congress that led to polarization within the general public.

Our findings support the conclusion that there are two clearly distinct visions of the good society. Polarization characterized the voting on nearly all issues coming before Congress in recent years. That much is now well known. Our research highlights the role that religion played and continues to play in congressional voting.

In chapter 2 we noted Demerath's (1995) insightful essay extolling the contributions made to American culture by Liberal Protestantism. However, in a broader context, Demerath pointed to the paradox that as millions of

Americans of all religions (and no religion) internalized values like personal autonomy and respect for the other, Liberal Protestantism was shedding members by the millions. Our analysis of changes in the religious composition of the House and Senate over the past fifty years implies that the loss of Liberal (and Moderate) Protestants from the two parties was accompanied by the loss of the core values Demerath saw as so important to American culture. As a result, we argue, compromise leading to bipartisan legislation has lost out to extremism. Our findings suggest that the center does not hold without the presence of Liberal and Moderate Protestants, or people in both parties who share those values. The contrast in the following paragraphs between Paul Ryan and Joe Biden illustrate the growing gulf between the parties.

In the 2012 presidential election, a Catholic, Paul Ryan (R-WI), was the first Republican to articulate his understanding of Catholic social teachings. Ryan argued that the teaching on subsidiarity meant that we should solve problems at the lowest level possible, beginning with the family and then look to churches and other charitable and civic organizations at the local level. He added, "The preferential option for the poor, which is one of the primary tenants [*sic*] of Catholic social teaching, means don't keep people poor, don't make people dependent on government so that they [don't] stay stuck [in] their station in life. Help people get out of poverty out onto [*sic*] life of independence," which cannot occur when the people look to the federal government for help (interview with Christian Broadcasting Network, April 12, 2012). In addition, Ryan strongly opposed both abortion and homosexuality. His values exemplify a Catholic fundamentalism that has much in common with the Evangelicals in the Republican Party.[2]

On the other side of the 2012 campaign, Vice President Joe Biden (also a Catholic) actively proclaimed the moral responsibility of government to reach out to those in need and reminded the voting public that Democrats had been doing this since FDR with Social Security, the G.I. Bill, Medicare, Medicaid, and now the Affordable Care Act.

Our data support the conclusion that both political parties have important roots in religion. The Republican Party slowly moved away from a Mainline Protestantism that emphasized personal autonomy and individual initiative as well as a recognition of the need to work across the aisle with like-minded Democrats to achieve compromises that assured that the center would hold. However, the moderate wing of the Republican Party has slowly disappeared from both the House and the Senate, so that now the orthodox coalition that Hunter had noted in 1991 has gained effective control of the party. Meanwhile, national polls during 2011 and 2012 repeatedly informed us that the great majority of Americans were disillusioned with Congress. Yet there was no sign that the same public intended to or could replace the members who were most responsible for the votes that reflected the polarization. Within the Republican Party those in the far right had control over many of the primaries. As the Republicans for Choice said in a recent article, "If the current environment within the Republican Party is hostile to choice, then it is the result of a deliberate strategy—convincing Republican candidates for office that they had to adopt an anti-choice position to get elected" ("Prochoice Republicanism" 2011). Gerrymandering has also contributed to the problem, according to Connie Morella, a former Republican moderate from Maryland, "referring to the practice of creating ideologically pure districts where the race is basically won or lost in the primary" (Morella 2012).

We also found that the roots of the Democratic Party are grounded in the Abrahamic tradition—the tradition that began in Genesis when Abraham welcomed strangers to his house and fed them well. The Jewish prophets have built on this tradition of not turning their backs to strangers, instead emphasizing the virtues of love and compassion, all the way to Jesus and later to Muhammad. In the words of a rabbi in Evanston, Illinois, "We are doers of social justice, not theologians." This was supported by the Jones-Cox survey on Jewish values, in which 80 percent of the respondents reported that social justice was one of their core values. Among Mainline Protestants, the tradition goes back a century to a lifestyle based on the "Social Gospel." Jim Wallis of *Sojourners* magazine has been a leading voice for government funding "to feed the hungry, clothe the naked, and find shelter for the homeless."

Among Roman Catholics, the modern tradition began with Pope Leo XIII, with all popes emphasizing the church's social justice teachings, combining the principles of subsidiarity with those of solidarity, the latter meaning using the resources at the highest level of government, when necessary. The data from Poole and Rosenthal make clear that Jews, Catholics, black Conservative Protestants, and Mainline Protestants today, as in the past, continue to lead the way in passing the social legislation that we identify with the Abrahamic tradition.[3] We note that the two Muslim and Buddhist members of Congress, also Democrats, supported this progressive ideology in their votes.

It is also the case that the Democratic Party has a strong commitment to science and reason, which is compatible with its Jewish, Protestant, Catholic, Muslim, and Buddhist members who have a tradition of commitment to faith and reason. Some may argue that the Abrahamic tradition is more cultural and secular than religious. What we do know is that these values are deeply rooted among Democrats, both voters and the people they elect to Congress, just as the values promoted by fundamentalists in the Republican Party are deeply rooted among their followers.

In response to the argument that the Abrahamic tradition does not justify the Democratic Party's support for abortion rights in a pluralistic society, traditional Jewish teachings allow abortions as a means of safeguarding the life and well-being of the mother (though the Orthodox movement is less unified on this issue; see Pew Forum 2013). Mainline Protestant churches have a number of teachings that, while not always condoning abortion, allow for abortions under some or many conditions.

Finally, there is the Catholic position. The hierarchy has long condemned abortion, although only since Pope John Paul II has the condemnation been so absolute that it trumps all other issues. A majority of American Catholics look to their own consciences rather than to church leaders to help them decide on the morality or use of abortion as a choice (D'Antonio et al. 2013). We have also cited Governor Mario Cuomo's treatise explaining the obligation of a Catholic in Congress to uphold the law of the land.

In 1982, Benson and Williams demonstrated that the great majority of members of Congress were religious, mirroring those who elected them. Further, members acknowledged that their religious beliefs and values influenced how they voted. Our research supports Benson and Williams's findings in two ways: (1) we found the political ideology of both parties to be grounded in religion, and (2) we identified specific instances in which religious beliefs and values helped explain roll call votes (see chapters 4–6).

Benson and Williams also emphasized the idea that knowing a person was, for example, a Methodist or Catholic revealed little about their voting tendencies unless their political party affiliation was also known. Our study found this principle to hold for Catholics and Mainline Protestants but less strongly for members of conservative Protestant churches, especially blacks and Evangelicals; it was even less applicable to Jews. Increasingly, it appears that the party one belongs to, whether in Congress or in the public at large, is the one whose values and beliefs are the closest to one's own. Unfortunately, at present, there seem to be few values and beliefs that are shared across parties.

In chapter 1, we noted the concern expressed by DiMaggio et al. (1996) "that the social attitudes in civil society had converged as the attitudes of party identifiers had polarized, raising serious concerns about political parties in a pluralistic society." Our findings suggest that as long as the Republican Party in the House is dominated by Evangelicals, Conservative Catholics, and Mormons, polarization in Congress will exceed that of the general public. Despite Meacham's claim that the parties reflect the values of their constituents, the Republican primary process in fact skews congressional voting in a direction that does *not* accurately represent those values. This is also true for the Democrats, though to a lesser extent. Since religion has been demonstrated to have a larger impact on Democratic voting, it would seem that the Republicans have managed to more selectively pick candidates that reflect their ideological positions rather than those of the general public. We hope that this was not what Meacham had in mind.

Appendix A

Appendix A is available on the Rowman & Littlefield website:

https://rowman.com/WebDocs/DAntonioAppendixA.pdf

Appendix B

LOGISTIC REGRESSION: IMPACT OF PARTISANSHIP
ON SOCIAL ISSUES AMONG WHITE PROTESTANTS

Table B.1. Logistic Regression Predicting Support for Legalized Abortion by Year among White Protestants

Independent Variables	2008 ß	p	2000 ß	p	1990 ß	p	1980 ß	p
Democrat/Lean	1.063	**	0.593	**	0.532	**	−0.510	**
Republican/Lean	−0.551	*	−0.191		−0.074		−0.107	
College graduate	0.663	**	0.945	***	1.131	***	1.09	***
Male	−0.420		−0.358	**	−0.136		0.055	
Age (18–97)	−0.006		−0.001		−0.002		−0.01	**
Southerner	−0.389		−0.264		−0.386	**	−0.195	
Attend weekly or more	−0.804	**	−0.979	***	−0.951	***	−1.421	***
Attend seldom/never	0.316		0.607	**	0.419	*	−0.01	
Intercept	0.68		0.229		0.346		1.329	
N =	(302)		(711)		(841)		(815)	

*** $p < .01$, ** $p < .05$, * $p < .10$

Table B.2. Logistic Regression Predicting Belief that Same-Sex Sexual Relations Are Always Wrong among White Protestants

	2010		*2000*		*1990*		*1980*	
Independent Variables	*ß*	*p*	*ß*	*p*	*ß*	*p*	*ß*	*p*
Democrat/Lean	−1.237	***	−0.046		−0.443	**	0.274	
Republican/Lean	0.475	**	0.151	***	0.318	*	0.315	
College graduate	−0.62	***	−0.679	*	−0.764	***	−1.045	***
Male	0.402	**	0.23	***	0.114		0.666	***
Age (18–97)	0.013	**	0.015		0.01	**	0.017	**
Southerner	0.539	**	0.019	**	0.157		0.621	**
Attend weekly or more	0.84	***	0.448	**	0.615	**	1.174	***
Attend seldom/never	−0.267		−0.434		0.274		−0.324	*
Intercept	−1.764		−1.082		−0.597		−0.195	
N =	(761)		(1,170)		(700)		(811)	

*** $p < .01$, ** $p < .05$, * $p < .10$

LOGISTIC REGRESSION: IMPACT OF PARTISANSHIP ON SOCIAL ISSUES AMONG WHITE CATHOLICS

Table B.3. Logistic Regression Predicting Support for Legalized Abortion by Year among White Catholics

	2004		*2000*		*1990*		*1980*	
Independent Variables	*ß*	*p*	*ß*	*p*	*ß*	*p*	*ß*	*p*
Democrat/Lean	0.084		0.099		0.479	*	0.127	
Republican/Lean	−0.679	*	−0.346		0.355		0.375	
College graduate	0.337		0.585	**	0.947	**	0.83	**
Male	−0.537	*	−0.267		−0.482	**	−0.506	*
Age (18–97)	−0.008		−0.01		−0.013	**	−0.024	
Southerner	0.388		0.395		0.184		0.072	
Attend weekly or more	−0.715		−0.462		−1.174	**	−0.498	
Attend seldom/never	0.962	**	0.899	**	0.647	*	0.976	**
Intercept	0.705		0.414		0.616		0.63	
N =	(206)		(353)		(360)		(314)	

*** $p < .01$, ** $p < .05$, * $p < .10$

Table B.4. Logistic Regression Predicting Belief that Same-Sex Sexual Relations Are Always Wrong among White Catholics

Independent Variables	2010 ß	2010 p	2000 ß	2000 p	1990 ß	1990 p	1980 ß	1980 p
Democrat/Lean	−0.885	*	−0.695	**	−0.30		0.063	
Republican/Lean	−0.064		0.201		0.319		0.018	
College graduate	−1.041	**	0.044		−0.215		−0.486	
Male	0.796	**	0.471	**	0.769	***	0.101	
Age (18–97)	0.24	**	0.026	***	0.28	***	0.032	***
Southerner	0.39		0.505	*	−0.233		0.738	*
Attend weekly or more	1.312	**	0.33		0.175		0.647	**
Attend seldom/never	−0.389		0.041		0.003		−0.43	
Intercept	−2.941		−2.184		−1.671		−0.794	
N =	(294)		(480)		(287)		(351)	

*** $p < .01$, ** $p < .05$, * $p < .10$

Notes

CHAPTER 1: SETTING THE STAGE

1. Our story includes data from 1960 to 2010 regarding the changes in the religious composition of the U.S. Congress; 1977 to 2010 regarding roll call votes on abortion; 1969 to 2010 regarding other key roll call votes in the U.S. House and Senate; 1969 to 2010 regarding Poole's Common Space NOMINATE scores; and 1972 to 2010 regarding Protestant-Catholic attitudes on abortion and same-sex relationships.

2. The Gallup Poll of May 2, 2012, reaffirmed this finding, including in its statement the criteria used to measure degree of religiousness.

3. See, for example, Allen Hertzke, *Representing God in Washington: The Role of Religious Lobbies in the American Polity* (Knoxville: University of Tennessee Press, 1988).

4. The discussion in this section borrows liberally from William V. D'Antonio, Steven A. Tuch, and John K. White, "Catholicism, Abortion, and the Emergence of the 'Culture Wars' in the U.S. Congress, 1971–2006," in *Catholics and Politics*, ed. Kristin E. Heyer, Mark J. Rozell, and Michael Genovese (Washington, DC: Georgetown University Press, 2008).

5. Brint, 1992; Dillon, 1996; DiMaggio, Evans, and Bryson, 1996; Evans, Bryson, and DiMaggio, 2001; Mouw and Sobel, 2001; Williams, 1997.

6. Evans (2002b) used General Social Survey and American National Election Study data through the year 2000 and found that the evidence was even stronger that polarization in public opinion surveys might be a result of polarization within the political system. Mouw and Sobel (2001) focused on DiMaggio et al.'s finding that among the American public, abortion was the only issue that indicated a growing polarization in public opinion. More likely, the surveys of the 1970s–1990s may well have caught the time of transition from a time when the center held to one now in which it is in disarray.

7. Even at the height of the Vietnam conflict, John Brademas (D-IN) described the role of Congress to be to explain, justify, interpret, and intercede with the public and with each other to gradually build consensus that makes it possible to pass controversial legislation (John A. Brademas, "The Emerging Role of the American Congress," *Proceedings of the Indiana Academy of the Social Sciences*, 1968). See also Goldman (1973), chapters 6 and 8.

8. Rev. Richard McBrien, a theologian at the University of Notre Dame, wrote an essay on "the threat of Catholic Fundamentalism," July 25, 1985, *The Catholic Transcript*, 5. Soon after his column appeared, the United States Bishops' Conference established an ad hoc committee on biblical fundamentalism. In September 1987, the bishops issued "A Pastoral Statement on Biblical Fundamentalism" (for the full text, see *Origins* 17, no. 21 [November 5, 1987]: 376–77). "Fundamentalism," the statement pointed out, "indicates a person's general approach to life which is typified by unyielding adherence to rigid doctrinal and ideological positions—an approach that affects the individual's social and political attitudes as well as religious ones."

9. Source: sermoncentral.com, "Top 100 Churches," http://www.sermoncentral .com/articleb.asp?article=Top-100-Largest-Churches.

10. These real-life examples are supported by recent surveys. In "Chosen for What? Jewish Values in 2012" (Public Religion Research Institute, Washington, DC, 2012), Robert P. Jones and Daniel Cox found "at least 8 in 10 American Jews say that pursuing justice (84%) and caring for the widow and orphan are somewhat or very important values that inform their political beliefs and activity."

CHAPTER 2: RELIGION IN CONGRESS

1. Many Puritans were Presbyterians, while others were Congregationalists. Much of the difference had to do with how the groups were governed.

2. *Mainline* is used to designate Liberal and Moderate Protestant groups as they have been distinguished by Wade Clark Roof and William McKinney. Per Roof and McKinney, Liberal Protestants include Episcopalians, Presbyterians, and Congregationalists (United Church of Christ); Moderate Protestants include Methodists, Lutherans, Northern Baptists, Disciples of Christ, and Christian Reformed; and Conservative Protestants include Southern Baptists, Church of God in Christ, Evangelicals/ Fundamentalists, Nazarenes, Pentecostals/Holiness, Assemblies of God, Church of God, and Adventists. Mormons are also counted as part of the conservative group, although they do not consider themselves Protestants (Roof and McKinney 1987).

3. Representative Paul Ryan of Wisconsin told the Christian Broadcasting Network that it was his Catholic faith that helped shape the budget plan. In his view, the Catholic principle of subsidiarity suggests the federal government should play a minimal role in helping the poor. "Was Jesus for Small Government?" *Zionica Magazine,* http://zionica.com/2012/04/16/was-jesus-for-small-government.

4. Between 1960 and 2010, the Jewish population was estimated to have increased from 5,531,000 to 6,543,820, while its percentage of the U.S. population declined

from 3.08 percent to 2.1 percent. Yet in 2010, the number of Jewish members in the House had tripled to thirty, and there were twelve Jews in the Senate (Sheskin and Dashefsky 2010, 3 and appendix, table 1).

5. See page 163 and pages 170–71 for more information. In terms of Jewish self-image in America, Greenberg and Wald refer to the Jewish Public Opinion Study in which "35 percent of Jews call themselves liberal compared to 18 percent of non-Jews; 8 percent of Jews call themselves conservative compared to 26 percent of non-Jews" (Greenberg and Wald 2001, 170).

6. Jones and Cox (2012) report that "at least 8 in 10 American Jews say that pursuing justice (84%) and caring for the widow and the orphan (80%) are somewhat or very important values that inform their political beliefs and activity. More than 7 in 10 say that *tikkun olam*, healing the world (72%), and welcoming the stranger (72%) are somewhat or very important values" (5).

CHAPTER 3: RELIGIOUS COMPOSITION OF THE U.S. HOUSE AND SENATE, 1959–2010

1. There are about two thousand different religious groups with adherents in the United States. Fewer than twenty have at least one member representing them in the House or Senate. As of the most recent election, in 2012, the incoming 113th Congress will have the following distribution of religious groups: House: Democrats—17; Republicans—14; Senate: Democrats—10; Republican—7. The Democrats now include Buddhists, Muslims, and a Hindu in the House, and a Buddhist in the Senate. There are as yet no Republicans from any of these religious groups.

2. The following categories have been grouped: Conservative Protestants include Southern Baptists, all Evangelicals, Pentecostals, and Mormons; Liberal Protestants include Episcopalians, Presbyterians, and Congregationalists (United Church of Christ); and Moderate Protestants include Methodists, Lutherans, and Northern Baptists.

3. As noted in chapter 2, we have followed Roof and McKinney. Mainline Protestants are mainline in the sense that they have made their peace with science, rational thought, evolution, and a communitarian theology. The number of Mainline Protestants from Southern states has increased dramatically in recent years, an issue to which we will return later in the chapter.

4. Though Mormons do not consider themselves Protestants, we include them in the Conservative Protestant category because of their voting patterns.

5. Much of the growth among Southern Baptists is derived from the increase in the number of African Americans in Congress since the Voting Rights Act of 1965. Though their church theology is conservative, African Americans in Congress are consistently liberal in voting on social issues.

6. Some of the religious groups identified here, such as Christian Scientists, Eastern Orthodox, and Greek Orthodox groups, are not technically Protestant; however, they are included in this category because their voting patterns are consistent with Mainline Protestants.

7. Other Evangelicals are listed as simply Protestant, as in the case of Representative Todd Akin (R-MO).

CHAPTER 4: ABORTION

1. The Catholic Bishops opposed the Affordable Care Act on the grounds that they believed it could fund abortions. The Catholic Health Association supported the bill because their reading of it convinced them that it would not fund abortions. Anti-abortion Republicans continued to use the bishops' opposition to oppose the bill in hopes of weakening the public's support for it.

2. When *Roe v. Wade* became law in 1973, Medicaid covered abortion services until 1977, when the Hyde amendment went into effect. The amendment, which bears the name of House member Henry Hyde (R-IL), prohibits appropriated funds from being expended on abortion except when the mother's life is endangered by her pregnancy. Over the years, other exceptions for rape, incest, and severe health damage to the mother have been added, removed, added, and debated as the numbers of pro-life and pro-choice members of Congress have fluctuated. (See http://womenissues.about .com/od/reproductiverights/f/Hyde.)

3. Gallup polls over time, as well as recent Pew Forum polls, have reported a decline in the percentage of Americans supporting abortion in most or all conditions and a rise in the percentage supporting abortion only in some conditions. However, as noted in chapter 1, Jones et al. (2011) found that, overall, 57 percent of Americans continued to support a woman's right to abortion in some or most cases.

4. The religious affiliations of members of Congress are widely available on the Internet. Some lists include only the name of the member of Congress, with political party and religious affiliation, while others provide summary statements about the number of each major denomination. Some lists also include nonvoting members from Puerto Rico, Guam, and so forth. We include in our lists only those with voting power in either the House or the Senate.

5. Typical of the bills and amendments regularly voted on in the House and Senate were the following: allow Medicaid funding of abortions when the mother's life was in danger or the pregnancy was the result of rape or incest; prohibit funding of abortions in such cases; stop the District of Columbia from using any federal funds to pay for abortions; outlaw courts from ordering states to fund abortions with state money; stop federal employees' health insurance from covering abortions; ban military personnel and their dependents from obtaining privately funded abortions at overseas military hospitals (except in cases of rape or incest); withhold funds from international family planning programs that might include abortion counseling; and forbid certain late-term abortion procedures.

6. The religious typology used here is taken from Roof and McKinney (1987, 82ff; also cited in Christiano et al. 2002, 114–16), who divided Protestant denominations into three major groupings: Liberal Protestants, including Episcopalians, Presbyteri-

ans, and Congregationalists (United Church of Christ); Moderate Protestants, including Methodists, Lutherans, Northern Baptists, Christians (Disciples of Christ), and Reformed; and Conservative Protestants, including Southern Baptists, Churches of Christ, Evangelicals/Fundamentalists, Nazarenes, Pentecostals/Holiness, Assemblies of God, Churches of God, and Adventists. Mormons, who consider themselves to be Christian but not Protestant, are included in the Conservative Protestant category. Given the similarity in their voting patterns, we have combined the Liberal and Moderate Protestant denominations into one category called Mainline Protestants, following Roof and McKinney (1987) and Guth et al. (1997).

7. The voting scores are obtained as follows: each member has her or his own average vote score, determined by the number of roll call votes cast in each session. Thus member A would have a score of 100 percent pro-life if all of her or his votes in a given session were pro-life. If six of eight were pro-life, the average would then be 75 percent, and so forth. The average for each of the X number of House Catholic Republicans would then be totaled to yield the average for them for that session. The process is repeated for all sessions and separately for each sub-group.

8. For example, the following votes illustrate the difference: Medicare Prescription Drug Coverage (107th Congress, 2001–2002)—Senate: Catholic Democrats in support 14 of 14, Catholic Republicans 1 of 10; House, Catholic Democrats 71 of 74, Catholic Republicans 4 of 49. Oppose Permanent Tax Cut—House: Catholic Democrats 70 of 74, Catholic Republicans 1 of 49. Lift Cuba Sanctions—House: Catholic Democrats, 62 of 74, Catholic Republicans, 3 of 49.

9. The Catholic Health Association is the largest association of health care services in the United States.

10. There are at least two religious groups that lobby on behalf of the pro-choice position: the Religious Coalition for Reproductive Choice and Catholics for Choice. So far, at least, they have received little attention compared to the Catholic bishops and the Conservative Protestants.

CHAPTER 5: DEFENSE, TAXES, AND WELFARE

1. *The Almanac of American Politics* by Michael Barone, Grant Ujifusa, and others—published every two years by the National Journal Group (Washington, DC) beginning in 1971—is a rich source of data on members of the House and Senate, in addition to providing information about the religious affiliation of the members of Congress, key votes, and rating by a wide range of interest groups.

2. The compliance bill was designed to ensure that members of Congress had to comply with federal standards. This was a procedural matter that seemingly had symbolic significance but was never made into law.

3. See chapter 4.

4. Meaning that there was a 45 percent difference between Democrats and Republicans in their voting behavior.

5. With the exception of the period between 2001 and 2005, due to the events of September 11, 2001.

6. The figures for Jews in the House and Senate are not presented because of the lack of a Republican Party representation sufficient to make meaningful comparisons. The figures are presented in appendix A, and some narrative is provided in the chapter to briefly describe the voting pattern of Jewish Democrats.

7. Because there were so few Catholic Republican senators, it was fairly easy to have no votes in the 1970s.

8. Prior to 1980, there were very few Conservative Protestant Republican senators.

9. Abortion-related welfare spending votes were not included in this figure.

10. The persistent zero percent support of Catholic Democratic senators to decrease welfare spending was over the same period of time.

CHAPTER 6: DOES RELIGION TRANSCEND SOCIAL ISSUE VOTING?

1. See chapter 3 for the assignment of Protestant denominations to the various major Protestant categories.

2. Independents are included in the party with which they caucus.

3. Taking the difference of party means is a common way to illustrate polarization in the House and Senate; see http://voteview.com/political_polarization.asp.

4. For percent of Democratic vote share in the last presidential election we have data for all four decades; for the other district characteristics we have data for all decades except the 2000s.

CHAPTER 7: TOEING THE PARTY LINE

1. The authors would like to thank Amelia Thomson-DeVeaux, online communications and projects associate at Public Religion Research Institute, for carefully copyediting this chapter.

2. James T. Patterson, in *Congressional Conservatism and the New Deal: The Growth of the Conservative Coalition in Congress, 1933–1939* (Lexington: University of Kentucky Press, 1967), traces the beginning of the Democratic losses in the South to the late 1930s.

3. Note that the electoral clout of this constituency, however, has diminished somewhat as white Catholics have come to represent a smaller segment of the overall voting population. For example, white Catholics represented 26 percent of the general public in 1972 compared with 15 percent in 2010.

4. As noted in chapter 1 of this volume, DiMaggio, Evans, and Bryson (1996) found that between 1971 and 1996, polarization in public opinion was limited, manifesting itself most noticeably in partisan views on abortion. This volume tracks the progression of that polarization and adds to the analysis more recent data.

5. As noted in chapter 4, 57 percent of House Democrats' votes on abortion were pro-choice in the 95th Congress, whereas in the 110th Congress this percentage was up to 88 percent. Republicans in the House have retained their 1977–1978 pro-life stance. In the Senate, Democrats' votes went from 71 percent pro-choice in the 95th Congress to 87 percent in the 110th. Senate Republicans became increasingly pro-life: 52 percent of votes were pro-choice in the 95th Congress compared with less than 10 percent in recent congressional sessions.

6. To complicate this picture, Evans demonstrates that among Protestants and Catholics, there has been increased intradenominational sorting on the issue of abortion, with the religiously observant more consistently opposing its legality and less religiously observant more consistently supporting its legality (Evans 2002b).

7. Data for 2008 has been omitted because there were not enough cases to run an analysis of white Catholics by partisan affiliation in the 2008 National Election Study.

8. The analysis in this section demonstrates that white Protestants and white Catholics are becoming more polarized on the issue of abortion, but the evidence presented here does not address the degree to which these two religious groups are shifting their views to align with party leadership (Carsey and Layman 1998, 2002; Zaller 1992) or whether white Catholics and Protestants are changing their partisan affiliation to match their abortion attitudes (Adams 1997; Killian and Wilcox 2008).

CHAPTER 8: DISCUSSION AND CONCLUSION

1. William V. D'Antonio, Michele Dillon, and Mary L. Gautier, in *American Catholics in Transition* (Lanham, MD: Rowman & Littlefield, 2013), show how Catholics have moved away from church teachings and rely more and more on their own consciences on matters like contraception and abortion. See especially chapter 4, "Moral Authority."

2. Mark Rozell concluded that Conservative Catholics and Evangelicals came together due "primarily to opposition to the cultural challenge to 'traditional values.'" Pope John Paul II's vehement opposition to abortion, contraception, and homosexuality was admired almost as much by Evangelicals as by Conservative Catholics. This "alliance of convenience," as Rozell calls it, may help explain Mitt Romney's selection of Representative Paul Ryan as the vice presidential candidate for the Republican Party in 2012. Representative Ryan had worked closely with Representative Todd Akin (R-MO) and other conservatives to outlaw abortion in cases of rape. Rozell also questioned how long this alliance would endure. See Mark J. Rozell, "Political Marriage of Convenience? The Evolution of the Conservative Catholic–Evangelical Alliance in the Republican Party," in *Catholics and Politics: The Dynamic Tension between Faith and Power*, ed. Kristin E. Heyer, Mark J. Rozell, and Michael A. Genovese (Washington, DC: Georgetown University Press, 2008).

3. An example of this tradition occurred on October 14, 2012, at The Catholic University of America, where Jewish and Catholic leaders led an interfaith conference on poverty in which they called on presidential candidates to address the poverty issue.

References

Abramowitz, Alan I., and Kyle L. Saunders. 2008. "Is Polarization a Myth?" *Journal of Politics* 70 (2): 542–55.

Adams, Greg. D. 1997. "Evidence of an Issue Evolution." *American Journal of Political Science* 41 (3): 718–37.

Anderson, Leah Seppanen. 2009. "The Anglican Tradition: Building the State, Critiquing the State." In *Church, State, and Citizen,* ed. Sandra Joireman. New York: Oxford University Press.

Ansolabehere, Stephen, James M. Snyder Jr., and Charles Stewart III. 2000. "Old Voters, New Voters, and the Personal Vote: Using Redistricting to Measure the Incumbency Advantage." *American Journal of Political Science* 44:17–34.

Asmussen, Nicole. 2011. "Polarized Protestants: A Confessional Explanation for Party Polarization." Paper presented at the annual meeting of the American Political Science Association, Seattle, WA.

Barone, Michael, Grant Ujifusa, et al. *The Almanac of American Politics.* Volumes 1972, 1974, 1976, 1978, 1980, 1982, 1984, 1986, 1988, 2000, 2002, 2004, 2006, 2008, and 2010. Washington, DC: National Journal Group.

Benson, Peter L., and Dorothy L. Williams. 1982. *Religion on Capitol Hill.* San Francisco: Harper & Row.

Black, Amy, Douglas Koopman, and Larycia A. Hawkins, eds. 2010. *Religion and American Politics: Classic and Contemporary Perspectives.* New York: Longman Publishing Group.

Black, Earl, and Merle Black. 2003. *The Rise of Southern Republicans.* Boston: Harvard University Press.

Bottum, Joseph. 2008. "The Death of Protestant America: A Political Theory of the Protestant Mainline." *First Things*, August, available at http://www.firstthings.com/article/2008/08/001-the-death-of-protestant-america-a-political-theory-of-the-protestant-mainline-19.

Brademas, John A. 1968. "The Emerging Role of the American Congress," in *Proceedings of the Indiana Academy of Social Sciences.*

Brady, David W., and Hahrie C. Han. 2006. "Polarization Then and Now: A Historical Perspective." In *Red and Blue Nation? Characteristics and Causes of America's Polarized Politics*, ed. Pietro S. Nivola and David W. Brady, vol. 1, 119–51. Washington, DC: Brookings.

Brewer, Paul R., and Clyde Wilcox. 2005. "The Polls-Trends: Same-Sex Marriage and Civil Unions." *Public Opinion Quarterly* 69 (4): 599–616.

Brint, Steven. 1992. "What if They Gave a War . . .?" *Contemporary Sociology* 21 (4): 438–40.

Brint, Steven, and Jean Reith Schroedel, eds. 2009. *Evangelicals and Democracy in America: Volume II: Religion and Politics.* New York: Russell Sage Foundation.

Burstein, Paul. 2007. "Jewish Educational and Economic Success in the United States: A Search for Explanations." *Sociological Perspectives* 50 (2): 209–28.

Campbell, David E. 2007. *A Matter of Faith: Religion in the 2004 Presidential Election.* Washington, DC: Brookings.

Canes-Wrone, Brandice, John F. Cogan, and David W. Brady. 2002. "Out of Step, Out of Office: Electoral Accountability and House Members' Voting." *American Political Science Review* 96: 127–40.

Carmines, Edward G., and James A. Stimson. 1980. "The Two Faces of Issue Voting." *American Political Science Review* 74: 78–91.

Carsey, Thomas M., and Geoffrey C. Layman. 1998. "Why Do Party Activists Convert? An Analysis of Individual-Level Change on the Abortion Issue." *Political Research Quarterly* 31: 723–40.

———. 2002. "Party Polarization and 'Conflict Extension' in the American Electorate." *American Journal of Political Science* 46: 786–802.

Casanova, Jose. 1994. *Public Religion in the Modern World.* Chicago: University of Chicago Press.

Chapman, Tim. 2006. "Boehner Letter on Rights of the Unborn." Townhall Blogs, Capitol Report, January 17, www.townhall.com.

Christiano, Kevin, William H. Swatos, and Peter Kivisto. 2002. *Sociology of Religion: Contemporary Developments.* Lanham, MD: Rowman & Littlefield.

Cuomo, Mario. 1984. "Religious Belief and Public Morality: A Catholic Governor's Perspective." John A. O'Brien Lecture, University of Notre Dame, September 13.

Danforth, John. 2006. *Faith and Politics: How the "Moral Values" Debate Divides America and How to Move Forward Together.* New York: Penguin.

D'Antonio, William V., James D. Davidson, Dean R. Hoge, and Mary L. Gautier. 2007. *American Catholics Today: New Realities of Their Faith and Their Church.* Lanham, MD: Rowman & Littlefield.

D'Antonio, William V., Michele Dillon, and Mary L. Gautier. 2013. *American Catholics in Transition.* Lanham, MD: Rowman & Littlefield.

D'Antonio, William V., Steven A. Tuch, and John K. White. 2008. "Catholicism, Abortion, and the Emergence of the 'Culture Wars' in the U.S. Congress, 1971–2006." In *Catholics and Politics: The Dynamic Tension between Faith and Power*, ed. Kristin E. Heyer, Mark J. Rozell, and Michael Genovese. Washington, DC: Georgetown University Press.

Demerath, N. Jay. 1995. "Cultural Victory and Organizational Defeat in the Paradoxical Decline of Liberal Protestantism." *Journal for the Scientific Study of Religion* 34 (4): 458–69.

Dewan, Shaila. 2011. "True to Episcopal Church's Past, Bishops Split on Gay Weddings." *New York Times*, July 19, late edition, sec. A.

Dillon, Michele. 1996. "The American Abortion Debate." In *The American Culture Wars*, ed. J. L. Nolan Jr. Charlottesville: University Press of Virginia.

DiMaggio, Paul, John Evans, and Bethany Bryson. 1996. "Have Americans' Social Attitudes Become More Polarized?" *American Journal of Sociology* 102: 690–755.

Dionne, E. J., Jr. 2006. "Polarized by God? American Politics and the Religious Divide." In *Red and Blue Nation: Characteristics and Causes of America's Polarized Politics*, ed. Pietro S. Nivola and David W. Brady. Washington, DC: Brookings.

———. 2012. *Our Divided Political Heart.* New York: Bloomsbury USA.

Dowd, Maureen. 2004. "Vote and Be Damned." *New York Times*, October 17, WK-11.

Erickson, Robert, and Gerald C. Wright. 1980. "Policy Representation of Constituency Interests." *Political Behavior* 2: 91–106.

Evans, John H. 2002a. "Have Americans' Attitudes Become More Polarized? An Update." Working Paper 24, Working Paper Series of the Center for Arts and Cultural Policy Studies at Princeton University.

———. 2002b. "Polarization in Abortion Attitudes in U.S. Religious Traditions, 1972–1998." *Sociological Forum* 17 (3): 397–422.

Evans, John H., Bethany Bryson, and Paul DiMaggio. 2001. "Opinion Polarization: Important Contributions, Necessary Limitations." *American Journal of Sociology* 106 (4): 944–59.

Fastnow, Chris, J. Tobin Grant, and Thomas J. Rudolph. 1999. "Holy Roll-Calls: Religious Tradition and Voting Behavior in the U.S. House." *Social Science Quarterly* 80 (4): 687–701.

Fiorina, Morris P., and Matthew S. Levendusky. 2006. "Disconnected: The Political Class versus the People." In *Red and Blue Nation: Characteristics and Causes of America's Polarized Politics*, ed. Pietro S. Nivola and David W. Brady. Washington, DC: Brookings.

Fiorina, Morris P., Samuel J. Abrams, and Jeremy Pope. 2005. *Culture War? The Myth of a Polarized America.* 1st ed. New York: Pearson Longman.

Fleisher, Richard, and John R. Bond. 2004. "The Shrinking Middle in the U.S. Congress." *British Journal of Political Science* 34 (3): 429–51.

Froehle, Bryan T., and Mary L. Gautier. 2000. *Catholicism USA: A Portrait of the Catholic Church in the United States.* Maryknoll, NY: Orbis Books.

Gitlin, Todd. 1995. *The Twilight of Common Dreams: Why America Is Wracked by Culture Wars.* New York: Henry Holt, Metropolitan Books.

Goldman, Ralph. 1973. *Behavioral Perspectives on American Politics.* Homewood, IL: Dorsey Press.

Greenberg, Anna, and Kenneth D. Wald. 2001. "Still Liberal after All These Years? The Contemporary Political Behavior of American Jewry." In *Jews in American*

Politics, ed. L. Sandy Maisel and Ira N. Forman. Lanham, MD: Rowman & Littlefield.

Guth, James L. 2007. "Religion and Roll Calls: Religious Influences on the U.S. House of Representatives, 1997–2002." Presented at the 2007 annual meeting of the American Political Science Association.

Guth, James L., et al. 1997. *The Bully Pulpit: The Politics of Protestant Clergy.* Lawrence: University of Kansas Press.

Hall, John A., and Charles Lindholm. 1999. *Is America Breaking Apart?* Princeton, NJ: Princeton University Press.

Hertzke, Allen. 1988. *Representing God in Washington: The Role of Religious Lobbies in the American Polity.* Knoxville: University of Tennessee Press.

Hetherington, Marc J. 2001. "Resurgent Mass Partisanship: The Role of Elite Polarization." *American Political Science Review* 95 (3): 619–31.

———. 2009. "Review Article: Putting Polarization in Perspective." *British Journal of Political Science* 39 (2): 413–48.

Hout, Michael. 1999. "Evidence of an Emerging Link between Abortion Attitudes and Political Views." *Gender Issues* (Spring): 6–32.

Hunter, James Davison. 1991. *Culture Wars: The Struggle to Define America.* New York: Basic Books.

———. 1994. *Before the Shooting Begins: Searching for Democracy in America's Culture Wars.* New York: Free Press.

"Hyde Amendment." 1976. Authored by Henry Hyde (R-IL). *Congressional Quarterly.* From http://womenissues.about.com/od/reproductiverights/f/Hyde.

Inglehart, Ronald. 1977. *The Silent Revolution.* Princeton, NJ: Princeton University Press.

Jacobson, Gary C. 2003. "Partisan Polarization in Presidential Support: The Electoral Connection." *Congress and the Presidency* 30 (1): 1–36.

Jelen, Ted G. 1997. "Culture Wars and Party System: Religion and Realignment, 1972–1993." In *Culture Wars in American Politics: Critical Reviews of a Popular Thesis*, ed. Rhys H. Williams, 145–58. Hawthorne, NY: Aldine de Gruyter.

Joireman, Sandra F. 2009. "Anabaptists and the State: An Uneasy Coexistence." In *Church, State, and Citizen*, ed. Sandra Joireman. New York: Oxford University Press.

Jones, Robert P., and Daniel Cox. 2012. "Chosen for What? Jewish Values in 2012." Publication based on National Survey of American Jews, Public Religion Research Institute, Washington, DC.

Jones, Robert P., Daniel Cox, and Rachel Laser. 2011. "Committed to Availability, Conflicted about Morality: What the Millennial Generation Tells Us about the Future of the Abortion Debate and the Culture Wars." Publication of the Public Religion Research Institute, 4, Washington DC.

Killian, Mitchell, and Clyde Wilcox. 2008. "Do Abortion Attitudes Lead to Party Switching?" *Political Research Quarterly* 61 (4): 561–73.

Layman, Geoffrey C., and Thomas M. Carsey. 2002. "Party Polarization and 'Conflict Extension' in the American Electorate." *American Journal of Political Science* 46 (4): 786–802.

Levendusky, Matthew S., Jeremy C. Pope, and Simon D. Jackman. 2008. "Measuring District-Level Partisanship with Implications for the Analysis of U.S. Elections." *Journal of Politics* 70 (3): 736–53.

Lipset, Seymour Martin. 1985. *Consensus and Conflict: Essays in Political Sociology.* New Brunswick, NJ: Transaction.

Luker, Kristen. 1984. *Abortion and the Politics of Motherhood.* Berkeley: University of California Press.

Mann, Thomas E. 2006. "Polarizing the House of Representatives: How Much Does Gerrymandering Matter?" In *Red and Blue Nation: Characteristics and Causes of America's Polarized Politics*, ed. Pietro S. Nivola and David W. Brady. Washington, DC: Brookings.

Mann, Thomas E., and Norman J. Ornstein. 2006. *The Broken Branch: How Congress Is Failing America, and How to Get It Back on Track.* New York: Oxford University Press.

———. 2012. *It's Even Worse Than It Looks: How the American Constitutional System Collided with the New Politics of Extremism.* New York: Basic Books.

Mariott, David. 2005. "Righteous Roll Calls: Religion, Choice, and Morality Politics in the U.S. House and Senate, 1999–2002." Paper presented at the Midwest Political Science Association.

Masci, David, and Tracy Miller. 2008. "Faith on the Hill: The Religious Affiliations of Members of Congress." The Pew Forum on Religion and Public Life. December 19, 2008, noted in http://pewforum.org/Government/Faith-on-the-Hill-The-Religious-Affiliations-of-Members-of-Congress.aspx.

McBrien, Rev. Richard. 1985. "The Threat of Catholic Fundamentalism." *The Catholic Transcript*, July 25, 5.

McKenna, George. 2006. "Criss-Cross: Democrats, Republicans, and Abortion." *Human Life Review* (Summer–Fall): 57–79.

Meacham, Jon. 2010. "We Are All Co-Conspirators Now." *Newsweek*, March 8, 3.

Moore, Charles B. "How Did the Pro-Life Plank Become a 1980 Party Platform?" http://www.MooreReport.com/mrpl_plank.html.

Morella, Connie. 2012. "The Secret History of the GOP and Choice." *Conscience Magazine*, December 20, 2011.

Mouw, Ted, and Michael E. Sobel. 2001. "Culture Wars and Opinion Polarization: The Case of Abortion." *American Journal of Sociology* 106: 913–43.

Mutz, Diana C. 2006. "How the Mass Media Divide Us." In *Red and Blue Nation: Characteristics and Causes of America's Polarized Politics*, ed. Pietro S. Nivola and David W. Brady. Washington, DC: Brookings.

Nakamura, David. 2011. "Methodists Approve Same-Sex Resolution." *Washington Post*, May 29, regional edition, Metro section.

Patterson, James T. 1967. *Congressional Conservatism and the New Deal: The Growth of the Conservative Coalition in Congress, 1933–1939.* Lexington: University of Kentucky Press.

Pelosi, Nancy. 2008. "Pelosi's Understanding of the Church's Teaching on Abortion, and Her Position." Interview with Tom Brokaw, *Meet the Press*, August 24.

Petrocik, John R. 1996. "Issue Ownership in Presidential Elections: With a 1980 Case Study." *American Journal of Political Science* 40 (3): 825–50.

Pew Forum. 2013. "Religious Groups' Official Positions on Abortion." January 16, http://www.pewforum.org.

Polsby, Nelson W. 2004. *How Congress Evolves: Social Bases of Institutional Change*. New York: Oxford University Press.

Poole, Keith T. 1998. "Recovering a Basic Space from a Set of Issue Scales." *American Journal of Political Science* 42: 954–93.

Poole, Keith T., and Howard Rosenthal. 1984. "The Polarization of American Politics." *Journal of Politics* 46 (4): 1061–79.

———. 1997. *Congress: A Political-Economic History of Roll Call Voting*. Oxford: Oxford University Press.

"Prochoice Republicanism: A Roundtable Jointly Convened by Catholics for Choice and the Republican Majority for Choice." 2011. *Conscience* 32 (3): 14–22.

Putnam, Robert D. 2010. "Tuning In, Tuning Out: The Strange Disappearance of Social Capital in America." In *Controversies in Voting Behavior*, ed. Richard Niemi, Herbert Weisberg, and David Kimball. Washington, DC: CQ Press.

Putnam, Robert D., and David E. Campbell, with the assistance of Shaylyn Garrett. 2010. *American Grace: How Religion Divides and Unites Us*. New York: Simon and Schuster.

Roof, Wade Clark, and William McKinney. 1987. *American Mainline Religion: Its Changing Shape and Future*. New Brunswick, NJ: Rutgers University Press.

Rozell, Mark J. 2008. "Political Marriage of Convenience? The Evolution of the Conservative Catholic–Evangelical Alliance in the Republican Party." In *Catholics and Politics: The Dynamic Tension between Faith and Power*, ed. Kristin E. Heyer, Mark J. Rozell, and Michael A. Genovese, 27–42. Washington, DC: Georgetown University Press.

Ryan, Paul. 2012. "Paul Ryan Says His Catholic Faith Helped Shape Budget Plan." *The Brody File*, Christian Broadcasting Network, April 12.

SermonCentral.com. 2012. "Top 100 Largest Churches." http://www.sermoncentral .com/articleb.asp?article=Top-100-Largest-Churches.

Shah, Timothy Samuel. 2009. "For the Sake of Conscience: Some Evangelical Views of the State." In *Church, State, and Citizen*, ed. Sandra Joireman. New York: Oxford University Press.

Shelledy, Robert. 2009. "The Catholic Tradition and the State: Natural, Necessary, and Nettlesome." In *Church, State, and Citizen*, ed. Sandra Joireman. New York: Oxford University Press.

Sheskin, Ira, and Arnold Dashefsky. 2010. *Jewish Populatioin in the United States, 2010*. Storrs, CT: North America Jewish Data Bank.

Smelser, Neil J., and Jeffrey C. Alexander, eds. 1999. *Diversity and Its Discontents: Cultural Conflict and Common Ground in Contemporary American Society*. Princeton, NJ: Princeton University Press.

Smith, Christian, and Patricia Snell. 2009. *Souls in Transition: The Religious and Spiritual Lives of Emerging Adults*. New York: Oxford University Press.

Smith, Lauren E., Laura R. Olson, and Jeffrey A. Fine. 2010. "Substantive Religious Representation in the U.S. Senate: Voting Alignment with the Family Research Council." *Political Research Quarterly* (March): 68–82.

Strickler, Jenifer, and Nicholas A. Danigelis. 2002. "Changing Frameworks in Attitudes toward Abortion." *Sociological Forum* 17 (2): 187–201.

Stupak, Bart. 2009. Stupak—Pitts Amendment, "to prohibit the use of federal funds to pay for any abortion or to cover any part of any health plan that includes coverage of abortion, except in cases of rape, incest, or danger to the life of the mother." Passed by the House on November 7, 2009.

Sullins, D. Paul. 1999. "Catholic/Protestant Trends on Abortion: Convergence and Polarity." *Journal for the Scientific Study of Religion* 38 (3): 354–69.

United States Bishops' Conference. 1987, November 5. "A Pastoral Statement on Biblical Fundamentalism." *Origins* 17 (21): 376–77.

United States Conference of Catholic Bishops. http://www.usccb.org/whoweare .shtml.

Vega, Arturo, and Juanita M. Firestone. 1995. "The Effects of Gender on Congressional Behavior and the Substantive Representation of Women." *Legislative Studies Quarterly* 20 (2): 213–22.

Voteview.com. 2012. "Polarization of the Congressional Parties." May 12, http://voteview.com/political_polarization.asp.

Wakin, Daniel J. 2004. "A Divisive Issue for Catholics: Bishops, Politicians, and Communion." *New York Times*, May 31, A-12.

Wald, Kenneth D., and Michael D. Martinez. 2001. "Jewish Religiosity and Political Attitudes in the United States and Israel." *Political Behavior* 23 (4): 377–97.

Welch, Susan. 1985. "Are Women More Liberal Than Men in the U.S. Congress?" *Legislative Studies Quarterly* 10: 125–34.

Wheatley, Nate. 2010. "Is Religion a One-Trick Pony? An Empirical Study of the Impact of Religious Affiliation on Voting in Congress." *Res Publica—Journal of Undergraduate Research* 15 (1).

White, John K. 1988. *The New Politics of Old Values*. Hanover: University Press of New England.

———. 2003. *The Values Divide: American Politics and Culture in Transition*. Washington, DC: CQ Press.

Wilcox, Clyde. 2001. "Evangelicals and Abortion." Paper presented at the Evangelical Civic Engagement Colloquium, Cape Elizabeth, Maine.

Williams, Rhys, ed. 1997. *Cultural Wars in American Politics*. New York: Aldine de Gruyter.

Wolfe, Alan. 2006. "Myths and Realities of Religion in Politics." In *Red and Blue Nation: Characteristics and Causes of America's Polarized Politics*, ed. Pietro S. Nivola and David W. Brady. Washington, DC: Brookings.

Wuthnow, Robert. 1988. *The Restructuring of American Religion: Society and Faith since World War II*. Princeton, NJ: Princeton University Press.

Yang, Alan S. 1997. "The Polls—Trends: Attitudes toward Homosexuality." *Public Opinion Quarterly* 61 (3): 477–507.

Zaller, John R. 1992. *The Nature and Origins of Mass Opinion*. New York: Cambridge University Press.

Index

ABMs. *See* antiballistic missiles

abortion controversy, 43–62; funding issue, 44, 59–61, 138n3, 138n6; general public on, 44, 57, 61, 106–10, *107–9*, 125, 138n4; health care bill divided by, 2, 59–61; Hout's analysis of, 47; logistic regression on partisanship impact, *131*, *132*; party and religious affiliation in, 56–59, 123; party trumping religion in, 123; predictive power of party affiliation and, 114–16, 141n5, 141n8; previous research, 5, *7*, 7–8, 9; religious lobbyists and, 61, 139n11; religiousness and, 106, 141n6; Republican leaders supporting abortion, 45; Republican Party anti-abortion, 9, 44–45, 46, 122; *Roe v. Wade* background of, *7*, 42, 44–47, 138n3; voting patterns in, 47–59, *49–50*, *52–53*, *55–56*, 138n5, 139n8. *See also specific religious groups*

Abrahamic tradition, 127–28

Affordable Care Act. *See* Patient Protection and Affordable Care Act

African Americans: as Baptists, 31, 35; in Congress, 35, 100, 137n5;

ideology and voting of Protestant, 96–97

Akin, Todd, 141n2

alliance of convenience, 141n2

Almanac of American Politics, 43, 63, 139n1

Anabaptists, 23

antiballistic missiles (ABMs), 65

B-1 bomber, 65

Baptists. *See* Anabaptists; Southern Baptists

Barone, Michael, 15, 48, 63, 89

Benson, Peter, 3–4, 5, 17, 18, 19, 50–51

Beth Emet, Free Synagogue, 11–12

Biden, Joe, 45, 126

Boehner, John, 25, 51

Bryson, Bethany, 9, 12, 15, 57–58, 119–20, 125, 128, 140n4

Buddhists, 31, 137n1

Burstein, Paul, 26

Bush, George H. W., 45, 69

Bush, George W., 23, 38, 47, 71, 85

Calvin, John, 19

Campbell, David, 10–12

Cantor, Eric, 54

logistic regression predicting beliefs about, *132, 133*
Santorum, Rick, 42
Saudi Arabia, arms sales to, 68
Second Vatican Council, 25
Senate: 1959–2010 number and diversity in, 37–38; abortion votes in, 49, *50*, 54–56, *55–56*; Catholics in, 41, *41*, 121; defense spending votes in, 69–72, *69–72*; DW-NOMINATE regression by party, religion and controls, 97, *98–99*, 100; Mainline Protestants in, 37, 38, *38*; number of Jews in 1959–2010, 41, *41*, 121–22; party affiliation changes 1959–2010, 38–41, *38–41*; population representation relationship to, 41; pro-choice vote analysis, 58; tax bill votes by party and religious affiliation, 76–79, *76–79*; voting behavior differences between House and, 5–6; welfare votes by party and religious affiliation, *82*, 82–86, *83–85*. See also voting patterns, in Congress
separation of church and state, 20–23, 24
Shelledy, Robert, 25
Sheridan, Michael, 46
Sibelius, Kathleen, 59
social issues. *See* defense spending bills; partisan divide, on social issues; tax bills; welfare votes
solidarity principle, 25–26, 127
Southern Baptists, 29, 137n5; African American, 31, 35; classification, 22, 32; in House, 32; in Senate 1959–2010, 40, *40*. See also Anabaptists
Strategic Defense Initiative program, 69
Stupak, Bart, 59–61
subsidiarity principle, 25–26, 127, 136n3

tax bills: tax reform consensus status, 74; votes by party and religious affiliation, 73–79, *73–78*

tax cuts, 73–76, 78–79, 124
Tax Reform Act (1986), 73, 76
Third Plenary Council, 24

Ujifusa, Grant, 89, 139n1
underrepresentation, 38
Unitarians: party affiliation in House 1959–2010, *33*, 34; in Senate, 39, *39*
United States Conference of Catholic Bishops (USCCB), 24, 136n9

Vatican Council II (1960s), 25
Vietnam War, 65, 68–69
voting patterns, in Congress, 9; data source for analyzing, 63, 139n1; on defense spending bills, 64–72, *65–67, 69–72*, 123–24; House-Senate differences in behavior, 5–6; issues listed, 64; reasons for separating by chamber, 120; religious groups in research based on, 29–30, 137n6, 138n7; tax bills, *73–78*, 73–79; voting schedules of House and Senate, 64; welfare bills, *79–85*, 79–86, 140n10. See also ideology; roll call votes
voting patterns, on abortion, 47–49, *49–50*; data source for analyzing, 47–48, 138n5; House, 49, *49, 52–53*, 52–54; score methodology, 139n8; Senate, 49, *50*, 54–56, *55–56*
Voting Rights Act of 1965, 31, 137n5

Wald, Kenneth, 26
Washington Post, 89
welfare votes: party and religious affiliation, 79–85, *79–85*; reform programs included in, 79; Senate Catholics and, 83–86, 140n10; summary of voting patterns for, 124
Wheatley, Nate, 6
white Catholics: logistic regression on partisanship impact on, *132–33*; partisan divide between white Protestants and, 103–4; partisan

About the Authors

William V. D'Antonio holds a BA from Yale University (1948), an MA from the University of Wisconsin (1953), and a PhD from Michigan State University (1958). While working on his MA, he taught Spanish at the Loomis School in Windsor, Connecticut, where he also coached the wrestling team for three years. After two years on the faculty of Michigan State, he joined the faculty of the University of Notre Dame in 1959 as assistant professor. He served as professor and chair of the Sociology and Anthropology department from 1966 to 1971. In 1971, he moved to the University of Connecticut as professor and chair. In 1982, he took a leave from Connecticut to become the executive officer of the American Sociological Association, where he served until his retirement in 1991.

He received emeritus professor status from the University of Connecticut in 1986. In 1993, he joined the sociology faculty of The Catholic University of America as a research associate; he is currently a fellow at the Institute for Policy Research and Catholic Studies at Catholic University. He is the coauthor of nine books and coeditor of four. He has an honorary doctor of humane letters from St. Michael's College in Vermont and was a Fulbright senior fellow in Italy in 2004. In the fall of 2008, the Center for the Study of Religion and Society in the Department of Sociology at the University of Notre Dame named its annual award to the Center's Outstanding Graduate Student in his honor. In October 2009, D'Antonio received the Rev. Louis J. Luzbetak Award for Exemplary Church Research from the Center for Applied Research in the Apostolate (CARA).

Steven A. Tuch is professor of sociology and of public policy and public administration at The George Washington University in Washington, DC. His research interests include social stratification and mobility, racial and ethnic inequality, and public opinion. He is especially interested in racial attitudes, changes in these attitudes over time, and explanations for the changes. In 2010–2011, he was a Fulbright fellow at Jagiellonian University in Krakow, Poland, where he conducted research on the political and economic transformations in Eastern Europe. In collaboration with William V. D'Antonio and John K. White, he has examined the role of faith in congressional voting. His published works have appeared in such journals as *American Sociological Review*, *American Journal of Sociology*, *Social Forces*, *Social Problems*, *Annals of the American Academy of Political and Social Science*, *Sociological Quarterly*, *Social Psychology Quarterly*, *Public Opinion Quarterly*, *Social Science Quarterly*, *Social Science Research*, and *Work and Occupations*, among others. He is coeditor (with Yoku Shaw-Taylor) of *The Other African Americans: Contemporary African and Caribbean Families in the United States* (2007); coauthor (with Ronald Weitzer) of *Race and Policing in America: Conflict and Reform* (2006); and coeditor (with Jack K. Martin) of *Racial Attitudes in the 1990s: Continuity and Change* (1997).

Josiah R. Baker is assistant professor of financial economics at Methodist University and adjunct associate professor of economics and geography at George Mason University. His research interests focus on the relationship between public policymaking and its economic and cultural consequences, particularly as globalization has affected welfare, defense spending, and taxation. In 2004, he was a Fulbright-Hays scholar in Bolivia, where he conducted research on poverty, natural gas, and coca production. His dissertation, *Constructing the People's Home: The Political and Economic Origins and Early Development of the "Swedish Model" (1879–1976)*, examined the development of the Swedish welfare state. His publications include four economics textbooks—*Macroeconomics: Theories, Principles, and Issues* (2006), *Fundamental Macroeconomics: Issues and Policies* (2005), *Fundamentals of Macro Policy* (2004), and *Macro Policy* (2003)—as well as articles in *The Encyclopedia of Africa and the Americas* (2008), *Encyclopedia of the Developing World* (2005) and the journals *International Advances in Economic Research*, the *Political Chronicle*, and the *Southeast Latin Americanist*. He has also published newspaper articles in the *Washington Times*, the *Tampa Tribune*, and the *Orlando Sentinel*.

Alyx Mark is a doctoral candidate in American politics at George Washington University in Washington, DC. Her research interests include law and society, judicial institutions at both the federal and the local levels, and bureaucratic politics. Her dissertation focuses on measuring the tangible impact to one's civic engagement as a result of interacting with legal assistance providers and the development of the contemporary legal services environment. Alyx received her master's degree in political science from GWU and her bachelor's degree in political science and environmental science from Southern Illinois University–Edwardsville in Edwardsville, Illinois.

Robert P. Jones is the founding CEO of the Public Religion Research Institute (PRRI) and a leading scholar and commentator on religion, values, and public life. He is the author of two academic books and numerous peer-review articles on religion and public policy.

Dr. Jones writes a weekly "Figuring Faith" column in the *Washington Post*'s "On Faith" section. Dr. Jones served for six years on the national steering committee for the Religion and Politics section of the American Academy of Religion and serves on the editorial board for the journal *Politics and Religion*, a journal of the American Political Science Association. He is also an active member of the Society for the Scientific Study of Religion, the Society of Christian Ethics, and the American Association of Public Opinion Research. He holds a PhD in religion from Emory University, where he specialized in sociology of religion, politics, and religious ethics. He also holds an M.Div. from Southwestern Baptist Theological Seminary.

Before founding PRRI, Dr. Jones worked as a consultant and senior research fellow at several think tanks in Washington, DC, and was assistant professor of religious studies at Missouri State University. Dr. Jones is frequently featured in major national media such as CNN, NPR, the *New York Times*, the *Washington Post*, *Time*, and others. Dr. Jones's two books are *Progressive and Religious: How Christian, Jewish, Muslim, and Buddhist Leaders Are Moving beyond the Culture Wars and Transforming American Public Life* (2008) and *Liberalism's Troubled Search for Equality* (2007).

Daniel Cox is the director of research and cofounder of the Public Religion Research Institute. Prior to joining PRRI, he served as research associate at the Pew Forum on Religion & Public Life, where he worked on the core research team for dozens of polls, including the groundbreaking Religious Landscape Survey, one of the largest public opinion surveys on religion ever conducted. Mr. Cox specializes in youth politics and religion, and his work has appeared in numerous national news and religious publications, including the *New York Times*, ABC News, CNN, *Newsweek*, *World Magazine*, and others. Cox holds an MA in American government from Georgetown University and a BA in political science from Union College. He is an active member of the American Association of Public Opinion Research (AAPOR).